On the Bend of the Kentucky River The Archaeology of Bethel Academy

By

G. Herbert Livingston

Complied By
Robert A. Danielson

First Fruits Press
Wilmore,Kentucky
c2017

On the bend of the Kentucky River: the archaeology of Bethel Academy

By G. Herbert Livingston
Compiled by Robert A. Danielson.
First Fruits Press, ©2017

ISBN: 9781621716198 (print), 9781621716204 (digital), 9781621716211 (kindle)

Digital version at http://place.asburyseminary.edu/firstfruitsheritagematerial/140/

Livingston, G. Herbert (George Herbert), 1916-
   On the bend of the Kentucky River : the archaeology of Bethel Academy / by G. Herbert
Livingston ; compiled by Robert A. Danielson. -- Wilmore, Kentucky : First Fruits Press,
©2017.
            115, [11] pages; 21 cm.
            1. Kentucky at the time of Bethel Academy -- 2. The Bethel Academy story -- 3.
            Important men related to Bethel Academy -- 4. The spade uncovers Bethel Academy -
            - Appendix A -- Appendix B -- Appendix C – Bethel Academy: more important
            documents.
            Includes bibliographical references.
            A compilation of articles from the Asbury Theological Journal.
            ISBN - 13: 9781621716198 (pbk.)
            1. Bethel Academy (Wilmore, Ky.)--History. 2. Excavations (Archaeology)--
            Kentucky--Wilmore. 3. Church schools--Kentucky--History. 4. Methodist Church--
            Education--Kentucky--History. I. Title. II. Danielson, Robert A. (Robert Alden),
            1969- III. Asbury Theological Journal.
LC577.L59 2017

Cover design by Jon Ramsay

asburyseminary.edu
800.2ASBURY
204 North Lexington Avenue
Wilmore, Kentucky 40390

First Fruits
THE ACADEMIC OPEN PRESS OF ASBURY SEMINARY

First Fruits Press
The Academic Open Press of Asbury Theological Seminary
204 N. Lexington Ave., Wilmore, KY 40390
859-858-2236
first.fruits@asburyseminary.edu
asbury.to/firstfruits

Table of Contents

Foreword

Robert A. Danielson

Life in Archives and Special Collections can be interesting to say the least! I was trying to work on a publicity article for our institutional publication, when I thought it might be fun to look at the papers of G. Herbert Livingston, a former professor and archaeologist at Asbury Theological Seminary. As a trained archaeologist myself, I was hoping to find all kinds of interesting items in the boxes. But when they arrived, they were simply papers, with one or two boxes of odd Old Testament teaching materials and replicas. As I looked through the papers, I realized Dr. Livingston had been involved in a long-term excavation not too far from Asbury Theological Seminary. But where was the material from that excavation?

After consulting with the archivist, Grace Yoder, we got a key from maintenance to explore a huge storage area under the seminary's student center. We looked all over the place, finding nothing but dusty old furniture and damp boxes of institutional papers. Finally, I spotted what looked like a closet door. When we opened the door we found the archaeology lab of Dr. Livingston as he must of left it after his last excavation work on Bethel Academy in 1990, almost 26 years ago! The artifacts were still in their plastic bags, and the room contained map-making materials and archaeological tools as well as books and journals. It was an amazing discovery.

Over the next few days, student workers packed up the material and brought it to the archives. The plastic bags were beginning to disintegrate so we did a lot of re-bagging and reorganizing. As we continued to work with the material, I did the research to learn more about Bethel Academy and Dr. Livingston. In the process I found this amazing story, originally recorded by Dr. Livingston and published in a special issue of *The Asbury Theological Journal*, volume 49, number 2 from the Fall of 1994.

The more I learned about the significance of this site, personally chosen by Bishop Francis Asbury in May of 1790. In April of 1792 he returned to inspect the building and suggest some changes, but essentially the building was a smaller scale replica of Cokesbury College in Abingdon, Maryland, the first Methodist school in the United States. Bethel Academy would be the second, and first Methodist School west of the Appalachian Mountains. In 1793 Bishop Asbury returned to Bethel Academy, when trustees were appointed and listened to a sermon from the Bishop on the grounds of the new school. Classes started sometime in 1792 or 1793. We know nothing about how many boys attended, what their ages were, or what life was like in Bethel Academy. We do know that annual tuition was six dollars per student.

The life of Bethel Academy was short-lived, as was Cokesbury College, which survived from 1787 until it was destroyed by a fire in 1796. At Bethel Academy disputes arose, possibly due to the issue of slavery, and Rev. John Metcalf left Bethel

Academy and founded his own school in nearby Nicholasville before 1802. Rev. Nathaniel Harris was leading the school at Bethel Academy, but Rev. Metcalf insisted on calling his school by the same name. In 1804 Rev. Metcalf went and removed the furnishings of the original Bethel Academy without permission, and was suspended from the ministry for 12 months by the Conference in punishment. It appears that Rev. Harris had stopped actively teaching by 1803. Bethel Academy officially ceased operation in 1808, and the building stood empty until 1820, when it was torn down and the materials reused to build a school in Nicholasville. The cornerstone of Bethel Academy was removed and taken to Vanderbilt University in Nashville, where it was used in an outside wall of the engineering building.

While a form of Bethel Academy continued to operate for much of the 1800's in Nicholasville, this school was not tied to the Methodist Church. Bethel Academy as a struggling Methodist educational institution was temporarily forgotten until the building of Asbury College in Wilmore. Dr. Livingston's work and research on this site was extensive and deserves to be recognized once more. It is hoped that his republished version of Dr. Livingston's work will help continue the memory and significance of Bethel Academy into the future.

CHAPTER 1:
KENTUCKY AT THE TIME
OF BETHEL ACADEMY

G. HERBERT LIVINGSTON

When one is studying the history of a particular site, one should look at the context in terms of several factors: inhabitants, governments, migration patterns, as well as social events related to the site. This article will deal briefly with each of these factors.

Archaeological knowledge of the original settlers of the region known as Kentucky is largely confined to traces of structures in which they lived and were buried, along with a number of objects they made and used. These sites and artifacts indicate people lived in Kentucky for several thousand years, some assume as many as 15,000 years. They are popularly called Indians, though a better term may be Native Americans.

For some reason, Kentucky was largely abandoned as a home for these people for at least a century before white people began to move into the area. Instead, it became a "no man's land" used for hunting and fighting between northern Shawnees with their allies and the southern Cherokees with their allies. Their government was basically tribal, led by chieftains who were determined to keep all intruders out of their territory.

EUROPEAN CLAIMS TO KENTUCKY

Twenty years after Columbus discovered the Caribbean islands, Ponce de Leon found the shores of southeastern North America, and De Soto explored inland as far as the Mississippi River. The result was that the Spanish government regarded all lands south of the Ohio River and east of the Mississippi River as Florida.

At about the same time John Cabot of England located the northeastern shores of the same continent and claimed all of it for his homeland. When Englishmen settled in Jamestown in 1607, they called the area Virginia and claimed it reached from "sea to sea."

In 1524, Verrazano, the captain of a French ship, examined the eastern coastline and claimed everything that lay to the west of it for France. The first white men to see Kentucky were French led by La Salle in 1670-71, when the group explored the Ohio River by canoe. Two years later Marquette and Joliet made a trip down the Mississippi River and passed the point where Kentucky touches that river. In 1682 La Salle travelled to the mouth of the Mississippi River and likewise saw the western tip of Kentucky. He called the entire Mississippi Valley, including all tributaries, Louisiana.

These three claims meant that Kentucky was part of Spain's Florida, England's Virginia and France's Louisiana at the same time. Of course, these claims resulted in wars, especially between England and France. In American history these wars are called King William's War, Queen Anne's War and King George's War. None of these wars decided who really owned Kentucky.

After King George's War, the French showed their desire to possess all lands to the west of the Appalachian Mountains by building forts. One of these forts was on a site now known as Pittsburgh, from which they sought to stop English migrants from using the Ohio River to settle in Ohio and Kentucky. These forts played an important role in the French and Indian War, which England and English colonists won. This victory left England as the only European nation with a viable claim on Kentucky. The native Americans did not submit to this claim and fought invasion of their lands with vigor, e.g., the Mohawks. Some native Americans fought with the English, and many fought with the French in this conflict.

TAKING POSSESSION OF KENTUCKY

Technically, a few English people had visited Kentucky before the French and Indian War, but they were brought in as captives of Indians. They managed to escape and return home. Also, before this war, English hunters, traders and surveyors began to explore and exploit the animals and land of Kentucky.

Several land companies were formed to begin the task of surveying Kentucky, namely, The Ohio Company, the Loyal Land Company, and the Vandalia Company. The Loyal Land Company sent surveyors led by Dr. Thomas Walker in 1750 through a gap in the Appalachian Mountains which Walker called Cumberland Gap. He also called the stream just to the west of it the Cumberland River. At a site now called Barbourville, he built the first log cabin in Kentucky. The area he traversed contained steep hills and narrow valleys, which did not impress him, so he returned home.

The next year the Ohio Company sent Christopher Gist down the Ohio River. He found the mouth of the Kentucky River and moved up its valley to the head of the river, then went overland toward the northeast to the Kanawha River and on home. In 1754 James McBride, as a surveyor, travelled up the Kentucky River and across the Bluegrass region, known then as the "Big Meadows." John Findley, a hunter, was in the area at the same time and became acquainted with Daniel Boone during the French and Indian War.

It was several years later that Findley located Daniel Boone at his home in Yadkin, North Carolina, and persuaded Daniel and Squire Boone to go to Kentucky. The three men spent the winter of 1767-68 at the Breaks of the Sandy River in southeastern Kentucky but returned home disappointed with what they found. That fall, however, Findley talked Daniel Boone and four others into entering Kentucky by way of Cumberland Gap. They felt a sense of security because that year the northern tribes sold Kentucky to the English by the

Treaty of Fort Stanwix, and the Cherokees had done the same in the Treaty of Hard Labor.

Unknown to Findley and his party, many tribes did not accept these sales as valid and soon attacked and captured Boone and a friend in December of 1769. After the two escaped, the hunters tried to continue their hunt but one was killed, leaving Daniel and Squire Boone to continue on their own. After a short time, Squire returned home but Daniel travelled widely in central Kentucky. Over twenty other hunters also found much game in Kentucky, but often lost their furs to hostile Indians. During this decade, surveying parties were doing their work here and there in Kentucky.

James Harrod is credited with founding the first permanent settlement in Kentucky in May 1774. Travelling via the Ohio and Kentucky Rivers and moving inland, his party of thirty-one men began to erect cabins. Daniel Boone appeared on the scene and began a cabin for himself, but war with the native tribes broke out. After several months, the fighting stopped and a fort was completed at Harrodstown (now Harrodsburg). Meanwhile Boone was busy marking a trail with a hatchet, the famous Wilderness Road.

James Harrod was the founder of the second oldest settlement known then as Boiling Springs, but now called Danville. Another military leader, Colonel John Floyd, led thirty men to another spring, calling it St. Asaph but later known as Stanford. It was southeast of Boiling Springs on the Dick's (Dix) River.

Some of these settlers tried to get land titles from Virginia, whereas others moved on to the north and to the west, due to the threat of more Indian raids on their cabins.

The Transylvania Company was formed by Judge Richard Henderson of North Carolina with the goal of purchasing large tracts of land from the Cherokees and founding a colony in Kentucky. A treaty was made with the Cherokees in which $50,000 of merchandise was traded for the land lying between the Ohio, Kentucky and Cumberland Rivers, i.e., the south-central part and the western part up to the tip of Kentucky called "The Purchase." Daniel Boone was hired to oversee the blazing and clearing of a trail for settlers to follow into central Kentucky. It ended on the banks of the Kentucky River. After Judge Henderson arrived late in April, a fort was built and named Fort Boonesborough.

On May 24, 1775, a convention called by Judge Henderson met with delegates from the other settlements. The first laws of Kentucky were made at this convention and a document somewhat like a constitution was adopted for the Colony of Transylvania.

That fall Boone's wife and children, including two daughters, were the first women to settle in Kentucky. Shortly afterward other women arrived at Harrodstown.

In June 1775, men camped on the banks of Elkhorn Creek heard of the outbreak of the Revolutionary War and promptly called their camp Lexington. At the time there were about 200 white people in Kentucky, but in 1783 when the war was over, they numbered in the thousands.

During the war, many Indian bands led by English officers fiercely attacked the several settlements. Boonesborough barely escaped destruction. Many living in isolated cabins were killed or quickly moved out of the region.

The Transylvania Company sought legal recognition from the Continental Congress, but Virginia strongly resisted the move and formally declared Kentucky was a part of its Fincastle County. The Congress took the side of Virginia and the Transylvania Company went out of existence. George Rogers Clark put pressure on Virginia and in December

1776, Kentucky became a separate county of Virginia. Four years later, Kentucky was divided into Jefferson, Lincoln and Fayette counties. After much agitation and ten conventions, the Congress of the United States admitted Kentucky as the fifteenth state on February 4, 1792, and set June 1, 1792, as the effective date of statehood.

MIGRATION ROUTES AND DEMOGRAPHICS

In pioneer days, it was far easier to travel by water than by land, especially if the land was mountainous and covered by forests. The primary waterway touching Kentucky was the Ohio River into which flowed many tributaries draining Kentucky land. Migrants leaving homes in New York, Pennsylvania, northern Virginia, and other northeastern locations, floated down the Ohio River on boats and rafts.

The first significant stream flowing into the Ohio from the south is the Big Sandy River which forms the northeastern border of Kentucky. A few people moved up this river to establish homes, but the land was heavily wooded and except in the valleys, or "hollows," the land was infertile. Going down the Ohio River they came to a favorite port called Limestone (now Maysville) because people could go overland and soon enter the Licking River valley where land was less rugged and more fertile.

Farther downstream, across from Cincinnati, the Licking river entered the Ohio. This stream provided easy access to the northern part of the Bluegrass region and small settlements and farms soon dotted the valley.

Downstream the Kentucky River flowed into the Ohio from the south, and because of its size, could handle large boats and rafts easily. By way of this river, settlers could reach all sections of central Kentucky with their household goods and use it for trading activities.

The Falls on the Ohio River at Louisville, blocked further travel by boats and rafts, but people learned they could portage their goods around the Falls or go south to the Salt River. They could follow it west to the Ohio or to the east, to the Salt River valley's rich farm lands.

The other major migration route was overland through the Cumberland Gap at the southeastern corner of Kentucky. People could come down from the north through the Shenandoah Valley, from Virginia, from North and South Carolina, to this Gap and make one of two choices: They could follow the Cumberland River to the southwest through the Appalachians to the northern edge of Tennessee, or follow the newly created Wilderness Road through rough country to central Kentucky.

When the Cumberland River emerged from the mountains, migrants could turn up streams flowing in from the north and settle along the south-central part of Kentucky, called the Pennyroyal (Pennyrile) region. This area was settled more slowly than central Kentucky, which attracted most of the migrants. The Ohio River and the Wilderness Road were the most heavily used migrant routes.

In spite of the migration of many white people through Kentucky to the north and to the west, the first national census of 1790 lists the population of this area as 73,677, which included 12,400 slaves. Fayette County, with 8,400, and the most populous of the counties, stands in contrast to the 2,729 people living in the larger area between the Licking and Big Sandy Rivers, known as Mason County. In 1800, the population of the state was 220,955, with Fayette County still the most populous having 14,028 people. Lexington was the largest city in the state until the mid-1820s.

Only three men: John, Jacob and Samuel Hunter, are known to be living in 1780 in that part of Fayette County that is now Jessamine County. In that same year, Jacob became the father of the first white child born in the present Jessamine County. Some historians estimate that 2,000 people were in this county in 1790.

RELIGION AMONG THE EARLY SETTLERS

Most of the people who came into Kentucky were Protestants. The first religious service occurred on Sunday, May 28, 1775, near the close of the convention sponsored by the Transylvania Company at Fort Boonesborough. The service was led by Rev. John Lytle of the Anglican Church. The next service was held at Harrodstown conducted by two Baptist ministers who were invited by a Presbyterian layman. The first known Presbyterian minister in Kentucky was Rev. Terah Templin who came in 1780 followed by Rev. David Rice who organized churches in Danville and surrounding communities in 1783. Rev. Adam Rankin founded a church in Lexington. In 1796 a Transylvania Presbytery was organized and then divided three years later.

In 1781 three Baptist churches were started. One was near present day Elizabethtown, one in Nelson County and one in Garrad County. By 1785 eighteen Baptist churches were active in Kentucky.

The first Catholic mission was founded in Nelson County in the 1780s.

Two young preachers were appointed to Kentucky by the Methodist General Conference in 1786. They were James Haw and Benjamin Ogden. Both travelled and preached at a number of places in central Kentucky. The 1787 General Conference Minutes had the first tally of Methodists in Kentucky; there were ninety members.

In 1788 a Methodist pastor was appointed to care for 480 Methodists in Lexington and Danville. The next year 846 were accounted for; in 1790 there were 1,088.

Bishop Francis Asbury came by horseback to hold the first Kentucky Conference at Masterson Station near Lexington in May 1790. Two more circuits were added and pastors appointed to them. During that decade the membership grew as follows:

Year	Pop	Year	Pop	Year	Pop.
1791	1,392	1792	1,808	1793	1,907
1794	2,309	1795	1,944	1796	1,750
1797	1,797	1798	1,601	1799	1,737
1800	1,741	1801	1,631	1802	2,519
1803	4,171	1804	3,485		

By 1794 there were five circuits: Lexington, Danville, Limestone, Madison, and Cumberland and eleven ministers. In 1800 there were thirteen preaching places and eleven ministers.

In 1800 a powerful revival broke out in Kentucky and brought into faith a large number of people. This revival was marked by the appearance of a uniquely American phenomenon, the campmeeting. The revival began in Logan County at the Gaspar River Church under the ministry of a Presbyterian, Rev. James McGready. He was helped by two brothers, John, a Methodist and William McGee, a Presbyterian. The crowds became too large for the small log churches, so ministers constructed a platform from which they could preach in the nearby woods. Many people were converted to a vital relationship with Jesus Christ.

The Presbyterian pastor, Rev. Barton W. Stone, of the Cane Ridge Church near Paris, Ky., went to Logan County in 1801 to see for himself what was happening. He was so impressed that he returned to his church to hold a campmeeting-style, evangelistic meeting August 6-13, 1801. His success was remarkable and the practice of holding campmeetings spread throughout the frontier and continues with modifications to the present day.

Methodist ministers in Kentucky quickly adopted the campmeeting style of evangelism, and revival swept many into the Methodist churches throughout the frontier. It became a potent factor in the rapid growth of Methodism in the decades that followed.

SLAVERY AND ANTI-SLAVERY

Many newcomers to Kentucky came from Virginia, North Carolina, and South Carolina. Those who were affluent were slaveowners and naturally brought their slaves with them. Many of the people moving in from the northeastern states had strong religious convictions against slavery and were not timid in voicing their opposition to what they believed was a great moral evil.

The issue came to a head at the Constitutional Convention held at Danville after Kentucky was admitted to the Union in 1792. The constitution had to be drafted before June 1; it was completed by April 19, 1792.

Among the delegates of the convention were nine ministers led by the Presbyterian Rev. David Rice. They argued vigorously that Kentucky should not recognize slavery as valid, but they did not have the votes to sustain their views. They did have enough influence to modify the position of the new state on slavery. The constitutional statement is in Article IX. It reads thus:

> The Legislature shall have no power to pass laws for the emancipation of slaves without the consent of their owners, or without paying their owners, previous to such emancipation, a full equivalent in money, for the slaves emancipated; they shall have no power to prevent immigrants to this state, from bringing with them such persons as are deemed slaves by the laws of any one of the United States, so long as any person of the same age and description shall pass laws to permit the owners of slaves to emancipate them, saving the rights of customers, and preventing them from becoming a charge to the county in which they reside; they shall have full power to prevent slaves from being brought into this state as merchandise; they shall have full power to prevent any slave being brought into this state from a foreign country, and to prevent those being brought into this state, who have been since the first of January 1789, or may hereafter be imported into any of the United States from a foreign country. And they shall have full power to pass such laws as may be necessary to

oblige the owners of slaves, to treat them with humanity, to provide them with necessary clothes and provisions, to abstain from all injuries to them extending to life and limb, and in case of their neglect and refusal to comply with the directions of such laws to have such slave or slaves sold for the benefit of their owner or owners.

George Nicholas, a lawyer who lived in that part of Fayette County later to become Jessamine County, was a leader at this convention and vigorous supporter of establishing Kentucky as a slave state. When a second constitutional convention met in the summer of 1799, he tried strenuously to have his way but Article IX remained the same.

During this time, the strongest opposition to slavery centered in the Baptist, Presbyterian, and Methodist ministry and congregations.

Kentucky was a wild frontier when Bethel Academy was constructed. People were flooding in from Virginia and the Carolinas through the Cumberland Gap, and from the Northeast via the Ohio River, so that cultures from the North and the South mingled. Most of the migrants had little to no formal education; their interest was in land. A number of the migrants moved on to new frontiers, making it difficult to establish stable congregations, and to persuade parents to place their sons in schools for any length of time.

The migrants had practical skills in building, but little money. These skills were used to good effect in erecting the building in which Bethel Academy was housed, but provided little capital with which to operate and maintain a school. These factors, combined with the controversy about slavery, doomed the school by the Kentucky River, but it did not prevent it from reviving again and functioning for most of the nineteenth century in Nicholasville, Kentucky.

BIBLIOGRAPHY
1. Allen, William B.A., *History of Kentucky* (Louisville: Bradley & Gilbert, Pub., 1872).
2. Bobley, Temple, *History of Kentucky*, *vol. 1* (Chicago: The S. J. Clarke Pub. Co., 1928).
3. Connelley, W.E. and Coulter, E. M., *History of Kentucky, vol. 1* (Chicago: the American Historical Society, 1922).
4. Van Hook, Joseph O., *The Kentucky Story* (Norman, Okla.: Publishing Corporation, 1974).

CHAPTER 2:
THE BETHEL ACADEMY STORY

G. HERBERT LIVINGSTON

One of Bishop Francis Asbury's primary goals was to establish denomination-al schools in the various regions where the Methodist Church was active. The church growth possibilities west of the Appalachian Mountains impressed upon him the need of a school somewhere in that region.

The ministers and laymen in Kentucky, the western extension of Virginia, also felt a need for a school. The Legislature of Virginia, in 1780, decided to set aside escheated lands. These lands were property taken from Tories in Kentucky, who supported England, and were to be used for the support of pub-lic schools. Income from these lands helped establish Transylvania Seminary in Lexington, Kentucky. In 1783 the trustees of the seminary finally met to select faculty and decide on curriculum. Soon the school was opened for the instruc-tion of young men.[1]

In reaction to the establishment of Transylvania Seminary, Methodist laymen sent a message to Dr. Thomas Coke who was holding a conference in North Carolina in 1789. The message requested that a college be built in Kentucky and contained an offer to obtain three to four thousand acres to support it. This request was discussed at the conference and the response was that five thousand acres would be needed for a possible construction of a college within ten years.[2]

The people in Kentucky turned next to Bishop Asbury. Rev. Francis Poythress, the presiding elder (superintendent) of Kentucky, sent a letter which Bishop Asbury received in eastern Tennessee. Asbury refers to this letter in his journal entry of April 7, 1790, and in the entry for April 17, states he started on a trip by horseback to Kentucky and stayed at a designated place two weeks waiting for a band of men from Kentucky.[3]

His May 5 entry refers to a dream in which he saw Kentucky men coming toward him. The next morning while having devotions he saw two men, Peter Massie and John Clark approaching him. They took the Bishop to meet eight other men. After reading letters they brought and praying for guidance, the Bishop consented to go with them to Kentucky. At Valley Station more men joined the party, making a total of eighteen, most of whom were armed with rifles. Together they followed the Wilderness Road to Lexington in central Kentucky, arriving May 13.

At Masterson Station, five miles west of Lexington, was the first Methodist meeting house built in Kentucky. It was here that Bishop Asbury held the first Methodist conference in the area May 13 through the 16th. Six preachers made up the conference membership but others observed the proceedings. The significant action of the conference was a decision to establish (Asbury uses the word "fix") a school to be called Bethel and the raising of about three hundred dollars to fund it.

A layman at the conference, John Lewis, offered to provide one hundred acres on the banks of the Kentucky River as a site for the school. On May 17, Bishop Asbury and Lewis rode about twenty-five miles south to look at the land where the school was to be built.

As presiding elder of the new Kentucky conference, Rev. Francis Poythress carried the burden of collecting funds and organizing volunteer labor to construct a building. It was a monumental task, for money was scarce and no milled or manufactured materials were available in the area. Stone had to be quarried from the limestone that lay near the surface of the ground, then transported to the trenches dug for the foundations.

Good quality clay lay just below the sod, so as the trenches were dug, the clay could be mixed with water from a nearby spring, molded and fired in a kiln that had to be constructed. Thus thousands of bricks were made for the main structure. The kiln also reduced the limestone blocks to lime for the mortar and plaster needed. Trees had to be felled, providing branches to fire the kiln and trunks to be sawn and trimmed for beams, lathe, planks and shingles, as well as boards for making windows and doors. The thin glass for windows probably had to be hauled over hundreds of rough miles by mule back or by wagon, from Virginia, or by boat on the Ohio and Kentucky Rivers. No wonder it took four years to enclose the building and finish the rooms on the first floor. More details will be provided in the article on the excavation of Bethel Academy from 1965 to 1990.

Bishop Asbury returned to Bethel Academy on April 23, 1792, where he inspected the building and made some changes in the construction plans.

The Bishop returned again on April 23, 1793, and held a conference at Lexington from April 30-May 2, at which time trustees for Bethel Academy were appointed. On May 4 he met with these men on the grounds of the school, then preached to them the next day, Sunday, May 5.

The original trustees of Bethel Academy are named in the earliest deed for the property given by John Lewis, dated November 28, 1797. The grantee of the deed is "Reverend Francis Poythress now President of Bethel School..." and reference is made to an agreement John Lewis made with the trustees on May 16, 1794. Besides Poythress, their names are James Hord, Nathaniel Harris and Andrew Hynes.[4]

The exact date of the opening of Bethel Academy for students is uncertain. The problem is the date of a letter sent by Rev. John Metcalf to George Nicholas, a prominent lawyer in Fayette County and a friend as well as a legal advisor to Metcalf. There are three printed versions of this letter. One version of the letter was possessed by Samuel M. Duncan, who lived in Nicholasville, Kentucky. He claimed it was the original letter. It reads thus:[5]

Jessamine County, Ky., Jan. 13, 1794.

Honorable George Nichols:
I have lately received from you two of your kind letters, and would have answered them before now, but I have taken charge of Bethel Academy, and have been so confined for the last two weeks in fitting up suitable places of abode for some of my pupils, that I have greatly neglected my private affairs, and especially that portion of it which you are attending to in Lexington.

Your friend,
John Metcalf.

The second version of the published letter reads:[6]

January 14, 1794,

Hon. Geo. Nicholas:
I have lately received from you two of your kind letters and would have answered them before now, but I have taken charge of Bethel Academy and have been so confined for the last two weeks in fitting up suitable places of abode for some of my pupils that I have greatly neglected my private affairs, and especially that portion of them which you are attending to in Lexington.

The third version reads:[7]

Nicholasville, Jessamine Co., Ky.
June 13, 1794.

Hon. George Nicholas:
I have lately received from you two of your kind letters and would have answered them before now, but I have taken charge of Bethel Academy and I have been so confined for the last two weeks in fitting up suitable places of abode for some of my pupils that I have greatly neglected my private affairs, especially that portion of it which you are attending to in Lexington.

Your friend,
John Metcalf.

Besides the obvious difference of Jan. 13, Jan. 14, and June 13, in the date of the letters, there are several errors of fact in all of them.
First, the name "Jessamine County" is an anachronism, for this county did not come into existence until the Legislature of Kentucky divided it from Fayette County on December 19, 1798. The division took effect February 1, 1799. Secondly, the name "Nicholasville" is an anachronism also, for the seat of justice for the county was not

established until the justices of peace met at the home of Jonas Davenport in Jessamine County on April 22, 1799. Their motion reads, "Ordered that the seat of justice for Jessamine County be permanently fixed on the lands of Thomas Caldwell and Chesley Gates on the Hickman road."[8] These lands had been surveyed the previous 16th of September by Rev. John Metcalf. Note this letter:[9]

Jessamine County, Ky.
Sept. 16, 1798.

Hon. Geo. Nicholas:
    It afforded me great happiness to hear that you had returned in safety and health to your family and friends. I expected to hear from you more frequently, but, I suppose, the multiplicity of care and business prevent your devoting much of your time to letters, save what you wrote to me and Joseph Crockett. But now that you have arrived at home I shall expect to hear from you soon and as often as usual. I must inform you that I have named our county seat Nicholasville in honor of you. I was all day laying off three streets to-day, and my nerves are very much affected by the severe labors in the wet weather. These being the circumstances under which I write you this hasty note, I fear it will have put poor claims upon your time, but I can not help it.

Your friend,
John Metcalf

The town of Nicholasville was not recognized on these lands until court action was taken on August 26, 1799. The significant portion of the motion of the court reads,[10]

    On the motion of Thomas Caldwell and Chesley Gates it is ordered that a town be established on their lands lying on the Hickman road, at the place where the seat of justice for said county is established, to be called and known by the name of Nicholasville....

Previous to this action there had been an argument about the name of the new county seat, but the suggestion of Metcalf that the town be named after his friend George Nicholas prevailed.
    These official actions indicate that the place names may have been added by the respective publishers of the letter. The date of the letter remains problematic, unless Duncan's claim he owned the original letter is taken at face value.
    It is true that winter would be a good time for boys to attend school in pioneer days, but muddy roads and inclement weather would have made it difficult to bring in needed furniture and equipment and an adequate supply of food, to say nothing about keeping a big building warm with six small fireplaces on each floor.
    The other error of fact is the misspelling of the name Nicholas in the first published letter. The body of the letter is the same in all versions except for a dropout of "I" in the third line and the replacement of "them" for "it" in the last line of the sec-

ond version of the letter.

The number and ages of the boys who came for instruction is unknown, but an advertisement in the *Kentucky Gazette*, November 22, 1794, for students for the next term lists the basics of reading, writing, arithmetic and English grammar taught by Metcalf. The annual tuition per student was six dollars. In 1795, Metcalf's new bride Nancy (Ann Peniston; father, Thomas Peniston; mother, Elizabeth Poythress) probably served as the cook and nanny for the boys who lived in a building with unfinished upper floors.

There is no existing document which details the daily life of a student at Bethel Academy, but Nathan Bangs[11] preserves the regulations of student life at Cokesbury College. These rules were probably a model of student life at Bethel Academy and are reproduced here:

1. The students shall rise at five o'clock in the morning, summer and winter, at the ringing of the college bell.
2. All the students, whether they lodge in or out of the college, shall assemble together in the college at six o'clock, for public prayer, except in cases of sickness; and on any omission shall be responsible to the president.
3. From morning prayer till seven, they shall be allowed to recreate themselves as is hereafter directed.
4. At seven they shall breakfast.
5. From eight till twelve they are to be closely kept to their respective studies.
6. From twelve to three they are to employ themselves in recreation and dining; dinner to be ready at one o'clock.
7. From three until six they are again to be kept closely to their studies.
8. At six they shall sup.
9. At seven there shall be public prayer.
10. From evening prayer till bedtime, they shall be allowed recreation.
11. They shall be all in bed at nine o'clock, without fail.
12. Their recreations shall be gardening, walking, riding, and bathing, without doors; and the carpenter's, joiner's, cabinet-makers, or turner's business, within doors.
13. A large plot of land, of at least three acres, shall be appropriated for a garden, and a person skilled in gardening be appointed to overlook the students when employed in that recreation.
14. A convenient bath shall be made for bathing.
15. A master, or some proper person by him appointed, shall be always present at the time of bathing. Only one shall bathe at a time; and no one shall remain in the water above a minute.
16. No student shall be allowed to bathe in the river.
17. A Taberna Lignaria shall be provided on the premises, with all proper instruments and materials, and a skillful person be employed to overlook the students at this recreation.

18. The students shall be indulged with nothing which the world calls play. Let this rule be observed with the strictest nicety; for those who play when they are young will play when they are old.
19. Each student shall have a bed to himself, whether he boards in or out of the college.
20. The students shall lie on mattresses, not on feather beds, because we believe the mattresses to be more healthy.

During this time, the land on which Bethel Academy was built was granted to the school only by a verbal agreement between John Lewis, the owner, and Bishop Asbury in 1790 and a verbal agreement between John Lewis and Rev. Francis Poythress, James Hord, Nathaniel Harris, and Andrew Hynes on May 16, 1794, (perhaps this date supports the fall opening of the school). A written deed was not drawn up until November 28, 1797, delivered to the Fayette County Clerk's office May 24, 1804, and recorded April 15, 1805.[12]

For several years the school operated without official endorsement by the state legislature. The act which recognized Bethel as an Academy, along with others, was passed on February 10, 1798, recognizing Francis Poythress, John Knobler [sic, Kobler is correct], Nathaniel Harris, John Metcalf, Barnabas M'Henry, James Crutcher, James Hord and Richard Masterson as trustees of the Academy.[13]

On the same day, the Legislature passed an act that granted to each academy named, including Bethel Academy, a tract of 6,000 acres west of the Green River. Each could sell one-third of the tract granted to pay for erecting buildings, buying books for a library or other necessary academic equipment.[14] The land seemed to be a significant gift, but land was so plentiful in the state and prices so low that the expenses of keeping the grant outweighed any gains. The original Bethel Academy functioned for only a decade at the most. A.H. Redford[15] claimed the Kentucky Methodist Conference withdrew its support of the school in 1804, but there is no action in the journal of the Western Conference that supports this assertion.[16] However, the crucial years for Bethel Academy were 1798 through 1800.

Several factors entered into the decline of the original Bethel Academy and its closure. Bishop Asbury mentions distance from settlements (Methodists did not cluster around the school to form a village), fear of Indian raids, shortage of funds and inability to attract able leadership, he also has a vague reference to "other people's conduct" without giving specific information. Several data seem to indicate that these problems centered on the instability of conference and school leadership and the slavery issue. We will discuss first the leadership problem.

Rev. Francis Poythress had been appointed presiding elder of the Kentucky area by Bishop Asbury in 1790.[17] After the decision to establish Bethel Academy, Poythress became the president of the Board of Trustees of the school and served in that capacity for eight years. The dual role of being presiding elder of Methodist churches, which were separated by many miles, and as president of a school that had to be built at an out of the way place in a dangerous, primitive frontier, was a heavy burden on his shoulders indeed.

Poythress threw himself into his task without reserve. In four years he saw a building constructed and completed inside enough for use as a school building.

The burdens of the task proved to be too much for him. By 1794 he began to show physical and emotional breakdown. The main source of information about this condition is the memory of one of his preachers and a trusted friend, Rev. Thomas Scott, known also as Judge Scott. At the request of Bishop Asbury, Scott came from Wheeling (at that time still in Virginia), in April 1794 to become a pastor in Kentucky and served for two years at Danville and Lexington. He then married and soon afterwards moved to Ohio.

After providing data about Poythress, Scott describes his leader, as of 1794, in this way:[18]

> His muscles were quite flaccid, eyes sunken in his head, hair gray, (turned back, hanging down on his shoulders) complexion dark, and countenance grave, inclining to melancholy. His step was, however, firm, and general appearance such as to command the respectful consideration of others.

Scott continued the description of Poythress by noting that in the latter part of 1794 and during the winter of 1795 Poythress seemed at times quite detached from life about him. From time to time Poythress would complain of headaches and stomach problems.

He would spend time in bed during the day and couldn't sleep well at night. His times of depression would last for hours.

Just before a quarterly meeting to be held at Versailles, Kentucky, on a Saturday, Poythress asked Scott to take charge of the meeting. Poythress said he was ill and had to go to bed. After the meeting Poythress told Scott that Susannah Pryor (Poythress' sister), Willis Green, and Simon Adams were in a conspiracy against him.

According to Poythress, his sister was accusing him of not turning over to her all the money her brother had collected from the sale of several of her slaves; Green was saying Poythress had embezzled some of the money collected for Bethel Academy; Adams was accusing Poythress of dishonesty in a deal involving a horse. Poythress was sure the authorities were looking for him. Scott remarks, "During this conversation, his countenance exhibited a ghastly appearance, and his whole frame trembled." Poythress remained in bed with his head covered until Monday morning. Scott identifies this incident as an evidence of "partial insanity."

Poythress continued as presiding elder of the Kentucky Conference until 1797 when Rev. John Kobler was appointed to that position and Poythress was given a supernumery (inactive) status. However, Kobler left that fall for Ohio and Poythress finished the conference year as presiding elder. At the 1798 conference he was paired with Rev. Jonathan Bird as co-presiding elders over churches in eastern Tennessee.

Bishop Asbury transferred Rev. Valentine Cook from western Pennsylvania to Kentucky in 1798 to serve as presiding elder of the Kentucky Conference.

This is the same year Rev. John Metcalf decided the burden of Bethel Academy was too heavy and moved to a cluster of log cabins which was soon to be called Nicholasville. Here he built a log cabin and surveyed the first streets of the village.

In 1800 Kentucky was without an appointed presiding elder, but when Bishop

Asbury became aware of how ill Poythress was, he turned to Rev. William McKendree. McKendree was already appointed presiding elder of Methodist churches on the East Coast, but he was with Asbury, along with Mr. Whatcoat, at the October 1800 Kentucky Conference sessions at Bethel Academy. The Bishop changed his appointment of McKendree from the Virginia area to the Kentucky Methodist Conference. For several years McKendree served as presiding elder in Kentucky with distinction.

Meanwhile, leadership problems at Bethel Academy had come to a crisis point. After John Metcalf resigned as principal, Rev. Nathaniel Harris, now clerk of the trustees, placed this advertisement:[19]

A TEACHER WANTED
For Bethel School

A man well acquainted with the English, Latin and Greek Languages, Arts, and Sciences, who can come well recommended, will meet with encouragement by applying to the trustees, who live near the school. Boarding may be had in the school, for twelve pounds per annum; in the neighborhood, for ten pounds.

By order of the board,
Nathaniel Harris, Clk.
May 3, 1798.

Clearly, no acceptable response came to the trustees, so Rev. Valentine Cook, who had training in these areas of study while a student at Cokesbury College, was transferred from being presiding elder to the leadership and instructor position of Bethel Academy. Poythress became presiding elder of the conference again, but as Scott observes, "his bodily and mental powers gave way and fell into ruins."[20]

The next year, there seemed to be uncertainty as to whether Bethel Academy would open in the fall for another term of study. A letter written by Metcalf provides some information:[21]

Jessamine County, Kentucky
Sept. 9, 1799.

Rev. Charles Chenowerth:
    Dear Brother: Our meeting house is completed, and I invite you to be with us the second Sunday in October to preach the first sermon in the new house. I have written several others to assist in holding a revival, and am still living on the bank of the Kentucky river, and preach every Sunday.

Yours truly,
John Metcalf

Does this mean he was living at Bethel Academy, causing uncertainty as to who was in charge? Interestingly, Valentine Cook published an announcement:[22]

TO THE PUBLIC

As some of the friends of education have expressed a desire to know whether I designed to continue to teach at Bethel Academy—I think it necessary to inform them that I have engaged to teach another year, and am to begin the first day of next January; reserving to myself the liberty of going to the settlement at the time of the ensuing spring vacation, upon necessary business, to return as soon as possible. The price for tuition will be the same as fixed upon by the trustees in the preceding year, (with a very few exceptions) viz: forty shillings for common English, and four pounds, ten shillings for the languages, to be paid at the end of every six months from the time of entrance. None will be admitted for less time than a quarter; and if a scholar continues no longer he is to pay a fourth more, according to the science he learns. The parents may expect the utmost attention will be paid to their children's morals, without per-suading him to embrace any set religious opinions—in this I shall leave them to choose for themselves—I shall not allow one student to despise another for the sake of his religion, profession or sincerity—yet shall think it my duty to oppose those vices every Christian of any society would gladly oppose.

Valentine Cook

Cook ceased teaching at Bethel Academy after the quarter was completed and moved to Harrodsburg, Kentucky, to teach in a boy's school there, sometime in 1800. On November 9, 1799, he had married Tabitha (Tabytha, Tabby) Slaughter, whose parents lived near Harrodstown, now Harrodsburg.

Sometime during 1800 his widowed mother and younger children moved to a farm near the same village, the county seat, from Greenbrier County, Virginia.[23] Bishop Asbury records in his journal entry for October 4, 1800, that one of the concerns of the Kentucky Conference, over which he was presiding, was the future of Bethel Academy. A Dr. Jennings was favored as the next leader of Bethel and a letter was sent to him, however, he refused to come.

The trustees turned to their chairman, Rev. Nathaniel Harris, who agreed to move to the school building, The record is not clear, but it appears that he taught there for at least three years.

The "hidden agenda" that did the most damage to the welfare of Bethel Academy, and brought about its closing until about 1820 or 1821, was a sharp controversy over slavery among Methodists. Bishop Asbury never mentioned this issue explicitly as a problem for Bethel Academy. In the above mentioned journal entry, he vaguely writes of "other people's misconduct."

A check of several Methodist historians who mention Bethel Academy reveals gen-eralized statements. John Atkinson[24] in his discussion of Bethel, uses such phrases as:

"fiery trials," "complications," "influences that hindered," and "adverse fortune." Not once is the slavery issue mentioned. A.H. Redford[25] says of Bethel: "difficulties occurred which it would be needless to mention." W.E. Arnold[26] simply says, "We know the school did not prosper. Many things were against it."

To gain a broader perspective on this issue, it may be helpful to bring to the forefront some background information.

The years 1798 through 1800 were marked by political turmoil on the national and state level due to the passage of the Alien and Sedition Laws by the Federalists in the Congress and signed by President John Adams in 1798. These laws were regarded by many as violating the constitutional rights of trial by jury and freedom of speech. Quickly, the Republican Party adopted this position and became popular, especially in Kentucky, whose legislature passed the "Kentucky Resolutions," which were based on proposals first made by Thomas Jefferson. The Resolutions rejected the above mentioned laws as unconstitutional, and a similar set of resolutions written by James Madison was soon passed by Virginia. The result was that not only was Jefferson elected President in 1800, but after 1798 the Republicans in Kentucky pushed strongly for a revision of its constitution. A convention met in 1799, made revisions and set 1800 as the year the Second Constitution became effective.

George Nicholas of Fayette County was a Republican and as a delegate to the convention determined to renew his personal project of making Kentucky a slave state without qualifications. Rev. John Metcalf was an avid supporter of Nicholas and his projects. This action threw the Kentucky Methodist conference into turmoil, for there was a strong abolitionist sentiment among many of the ministers and among many of the laypeople.

In my archaeological work at Bethel Academy and my background reading, largely limited to the Methodist historians, I was not made aware of this issue adequately, until I read an unpublished article written by Dr. J.A. Smith, a pastor at Cowan, Tenn. This article is one of a series on early Methodist schools, some published and some to be published.

In this now published article, "The Case of Bethel Academy: Methodism's School for the Frontier," Dr. Smith brings the slavery issue to the forefront and asserts that this controversy was the real cause of the demise of the original academy. His discussion quickened my research into legal documents related to Bethel Academy. (See footnote 42).

I also began searching for and finding deeds, wills, and estate settlements in the Clerk of County Court offices of Fayette, Jessamine, and Woodford Counties here in the Bluegrass area. I was fortunate also to learn that Dr. Howard Shipps, professor of Church History for almost three decades at Asbury Theological Seminary, now deceased, had gathered five thick folders of research notes on Valentine Cook. They are now preserved in the archive section of the Asbury Seminary library. Data gathered from these sources support the theory that the slavery issue was indeed crucial to the demise of the original Bethel Academy.

Before looking at and evaluating this data, it may be helpful to summarize John Wesley's views on slavery and the changes that took place in the American Methodist Episcopal Church polity in the first twenty-five years of its existence as an organized denomination, in regard to slavery.

Wesley's first written statement on slavery is found in his journal under the entry for February 12, 1772. He makes reference to slavery by using phrases such as: "...execrable sum of all villainies commonly called the slave trade" and "...it infinitely exceeds in every instance of barbarity what Christian slaves suffer in Mohammedan countries."[27] Wesley published his significant essay, "Thoughts on Slavery" in 1774 and immediately felt the sting of bitter opposition. The text of this essay is photographically reproduced in a book by W.T. Smith who helpfully summarizes its contents.[28] The last letter Wesley wrote was to Mr. Wilberforce who had introduced a bill against slavery in the British Parliament.[29] He commended the politician for, "your glorious enterprise in opposing that execrable villainy, which is the scandal of religion, of England and of human nature.... Go in the name of God and the power of his might, till even American slavery, the vilest that ever saw the sun, shall vanish before it."

The two men Wesley sent to America to lead the Methodist movement (Francis Asbury and Thomas Coke) were just as anti-slavery in their convictions as he, and the young Americans who became ministers were likewise strongly anti-slavery. At the Baltimore Conference held in April 1780, the forty-two preachers gathered there wanted official answers to the question of slavery, for they were encountering opposition to Wesley's and the American bishops' views.[30] The minutes of that Conference preserve these questions and answers[31]

Question 16: "Ought not this conference to require those traveling preachers who hold slaves to give promises to set them free?" **Answer**: "Yes."

Question 17: "Does this conference acknowledge that slavery is contrary to the laws of God, man, and of nature, and hurtful to society; contrary to the dictates of conscience and pure religion, and doing that we would not that others should do to ours? And do we pass our disapprobation upon all our friends who keep slaves, and advise their freedom?" **Answer**: "Yes."

There was strong disapproval in the southern seaboard colonies to the affirmative answers to these questions and efforts of the ministers to carry them out. When Bishops Coke and Asbury preached on this subject and tried to put their views into practice, they met with excited resistance from most of their audience, and from some preachers. Only a few submitted to the requirement that they free their slaves.

The minutes of the Methodist Conference of 1783 addressed the problem again:[32]

Question 10: "What shall be done with our local preachers who hold slaves contrary to the laws, which authorize their freedom in any of the United States?" **Answer**: "We will try them another year. In the mean time let every assistant deal faithfully and plainly with every one, and report to the next conference, it may be necessary to suspend them."

Questions were raised again in the Conference of 1784 and answered as follows:[33]

Question 12: "What shall we do with our friends that will buy and sell slaves?"

Answer: "If they buy with no other design than to hold them as slaves, and have been previously warned, they shall be expelled, and permitted to sell on no consideration."

Question 13: "What shall we do with our local preachers who will not emancipate their slaves in the States where the laws admit it?" Answer: "Try those in Virginia another year, and suspend the preachers in Maryland, Delaware, Pennsylvania and New Jersey."

When the Methodist Episcopal Church was organized late in 1784, the following questions were asked and answered:[34]

Question 42: "What methods can we take to extirpate slavery?" Answer: "We are deeply conscious of the impropriety of making new terms of communion for a religious society already established, except on the most pressing occasion: and such we esteem the practice of holding our fellow-creatures in slavery. We view it contrary to the golden law of God on which hang all the law and the prophets, and the inalienable rights of mankind, as well as every principle of the revolution, to hold in the deepest debasement, in a more abject slavery than is perhaps to be found in any of the world except America, so many souls that are all capable of the image of God.

"We therefore think it is our bounden duty to take immediately some effectual methods to extirpate this abomination from among us: and for that purpose we add the following to the rules of our society, viz.: 1. Every member of our society who has slaves in his possession, shall, within twelve months after notice given to him by the assistant (which notice the assistant is required immediately, and without delay, to give in their respective circuits,) legally execute and record an instrument whereby he emancipates and sets free every slave in his possession who is between the ages of forty and forty-five immediately, or at the farthest when they arrive at the age of forty-five.

"And every slave who is between the ages of twenty-five and forty immediately, or at farthest, at the expiration of five years from the date of the said instrument.

"And every slave who is between the ages of twenty and twenty-five immediately, or at farthest, when they arrive at the age of thirty.

"And every slave under the age of twenty as soon as they arrive at the age of twenty-five at farthest.

"And every infant born in slavery after the above-mentioned rules are complied with, immediately on its birth.

"2. Every assistant shall keep a journal, in which he shall regularly minute down the names and ages of all the slaves belonging to all the masters in his respective circuit, and also the date of every instrument executed and recorded for the manumission of the slaves, with the name of the court, book, and folio, in which said instruments respectively shall have been recorded: which journal shall be handed down in each circuit to the succeeding assistants.

"3. In consideration that these rules form a new term of communion, every person concerned, who will not comply with them, shall have liberty quietly to withdraw himself from our society within the twelve months succeeding the notice given as aforesaid: otherwise the assistant shall exclude him in the society.

"4. No person so voluntarily withdrawn, or so excluded, shall ever partake of the Supper of the Lord with the Methodists, till he complies with the above requisitions.

"5. No person holding slaves shall, in future, be admitted into society, or to the Lord's Supper, till he previously complies with these rules concerning slavery.

"N.B. These rules are to affect the members of our society no farther than as they are consistent with the laws of the states in which they reside.

"And respecting to our brethren in Virginia that are concerned, and after due consideration of their peculiar circumstances, we allow them two years from the notice given to consider the expediency of compliance or non-compliance with these rules."

Question 43: "What shall be done with those who buy or sell slaves or give them away?" Answer: "They are immediately to be expelled, unless they buy them on purpose to free them."

Slaveowners who had been converted under Methodist preachers and joined the church, for the most part, reacted negatively to these rules and created disturbances wherever preachers tried to enforce them. Consequently, in the minutes of the 1785 Conference, this statement was added to the Discipline of the church:[35]

It is recommended to all our brethren to suspend the execution of the minute on slavery till the deliberations of a future Conference; and that an equal space of time be allowed all our members for consideration when the minutes shall be put in force, N.B. We hold in the deepest abhorrence the practice of slavery; and shall not cease to seek its destruction by all wise and prudent means.

The General Rules of the Discipline were amended in 1789 to add the following items to those activities forbidden:[36]

"The buying or selling of the bodies and souls of men, women, or children, with the intention to enslave them."

The words "of the bodies and souls" were struck out of the General Rule on slavery at the 1792 Conference."

After 1792, legislation for the entire denomination was limited to actions taken by the General Conference. That body, in 1796, inserted the following questions and answers in the Discipline:[37]

Question 12: "What regulation shall be made for the extirpation of the crying evil of African slavery?" Answer: "We declare, we are more than ever convinced of the great evil of the African slavery which still exists in these United States; and do most earnestly recommend the yearly conferences, to the quarterly meetings, and those who have oversight of districts and circuits, to be exceedingly cautious what persons they admit to official stations in our church; and in the case of future admission to official stations, to require such security of those who hold slaves for the emancipation of them, immediately or gradually, as the laws of the states respectively and the circumstances of the case admit. And we do fully authorize all the yearly conferences to make whatever regulations they judge proper in the present case, respecting the admission of persons to official stations in our church.

No slave holder shall be received into society till the preacher who has the oversight of the circuit has spoken to him freely and faithfully on the subject of slavery.

Every member of the society who sells a slave, shall immediately, after full proof, be excluded the society. And if any member of our society purchase a slave, the ensuing quarterly meeting shall determine on the number of years in which the slave so purchased would work out the price of his purchase, and the person so purchasing, shall immediately after such date execute a legal instrument for the manumission of such slave at the expiration of the term determined by the quarterly meeting. And in default of his executing such instrument of manumission, or on his refusal to submit its case to the judgment of the quarterly meeting, such a member shall be excluded from the society: Provided also, that in the case of a female slave, it shall be inserted in the aforesaid instrument of manumission that all her children which shall be born during the years of her servitude shall be free at the following time, namely, every female child at the age of twenty-one, and every male child at the age of twenty-five. Nevertheless, if the member of our society executing the said instrument of manumission judge it proper, he may fix the times of manumission of the children of the female slaves before mentioned at an earlier age than that which is prescribed above.

The preachers and other members of our society are required to consider the subject of negro slavery with deep attention, till the ensuing general conference; and that they may impart to the general conference, through the medium of the yearly conferences or otherwise, any important thoughts upon the subject, that the conference may have full light in order to take further steps toward eradicating this enormous evil from that part of the church of God to which they are united.

In the 1800 Discipline these words were added:[38]

When any traveling preacher becomes an owner of a slave or slaves by any means, he shall forfeit his ministerial character in our church unless he execute, if it be practicable, a legal emancipation of such slaves, conformably to the laws of the state in which he lives.

The annual conferences are directed to draw up addresses for the gradual emancipation of the slaves to the legislatures of those states in which no general laws have been passed for that purpose. These addresses shall urge, in the most respectful but pointed manner, the necessity of a law for the gradual emancipation of the slaves. Proper committees shall be appointed by the annual conferences, out of the most respectable of our friends, for the conducting of the business; and the presiding elders, elders, deacons, and travelling preachers shall procure as many proper signatures as possible to the addresses, and give all the assistance in their power in every respect to aid the committees, and to further their blessed undertaking. Let this be continued from year to year till the desired end be accomplished.

The General Conference of 1804 made these changes in several paragraphs of the 1796 Discipline, such as Paragraph 1: "More than ever convinced of the great evil of the African slavery, which still exists in these United States," was changed to, "As much as ever convinced of the great evil of slavery." Paragraph 3 was changed by the insertion of "except at the request of the slave, in cases of mercy and humanity, agreeably to the judgment of a committee of the male members of the society, appointed by the preacher who has the charge of the circuit," between the words, "purchasing" and "shall immediately."

Also inserted in this paragraph were these words: "Provided also, that if a member of our society shall buy a slave with a certificate of future emancipation, the terms of the emancipation shall, notwithstanding, be subject to the decision of the quarterly meeting conference."

Words after "nevertheless," were replaced by "the members of our societies in the states of North Carolina, South Carolina, Georgia, and Tennessee, shall be exempted from the operation of the above rules." The part about petitions to state legislatures was replaced by the statement:

"Let our preachers, from time to time, as occasion serves, admonish and exhort all slaves to render due respect and obedience to the commands and interests of their respective masters."[39]

Then in 1808 all words that spoke to members holding slaves were removed and replaced by the words: "The General Conference authorizes each annual conference to form its own regulations relative to buying and selling slaves."[40] These quotations from the early editions of the Discipline of the Methodist Episcopal Church demonstrate the strong position of the General Conference against slavery, but also reveal the difficulties of enforcing rules on slave-holding in states that had stringent laws on their books supporting slavery.

The bondage of Africans in slavery was an accepted way of life in a number of the American colonies long before the arrival of Methodism on American shores. W.T. Smith summarizes the situation thus:[41]

> In 1641, Massachusetts became the first colony to give statutory recognition to slavery. This was followed in rapid succession by Connecticut in 1650, Virginia in 1661, Maryland in 1663, New York and New Jersey in 1664, South Carolina in 1682, Rhode Island and Pennsylvania in 1700, North Carolina in 1715, and Georgia in 1750. Slavery was, ergo, part of the fabric of American life and culture.

The firm abolitionist stance of the American Methodists in their earliest official statements was a bold challenge to an established culture in the states existing in the Union after the Revolutionary War. However, the Methodists soon found themselves caught in a painful dilemma: Officially, the new denomination was an outspoken foe of slavery, but many of the new converts were slaveholders who must free their slaves should they become members or preachers. On the other hand, the laws of the states mentioned above protected slavery, making it difficult to free slaves. The majority of the slaveholders deeply resented the demands of the upstart Methodist movement and resented the freeing of slaves by its converts. The freed slaves could generate a desire for freedom among slaves on many of the plantations, causing unrest, disobedience, or escape from bondage.

The innovative General Rule prohibiting the buying or selling of slaves, except to set them free, was met with the objection that if they were immediately set free, who would hire them, or if reduced to abject poverty, who would provide housing, food, and clothing? Even Methodist converts were persuaded by these objections. As a result, qualifications, even exemptions, soon appeared in succeeding Disciplines.

A review of the regulations laid down by successive Conferences and General Conferences, shows that allowances were soon made for obedience to the laws of the several states, and for a series of phases in liberating slaves. Thus it was possible for members and preachers to have slaves for years before all were set free. Concurrently, the General Conferences would publish strong statements against slavery and require the church leaders to discipline preachers and members who did not emancipate their slaves as quickly as they should.

How did this dilemma affect Methodism in Kentucky and affect the operation of Bethel Academy?

First, the prospects of a sharp conflict among the swelling tide of white settlers in the Kentucky section of Virginia over the legitimacy of slavery was bound to develop. After the Revolutionary War, the government of Virginia made generous grants of land in Kentucky to veterans of that war who served in Virginian armed forces. Many slaveholders received these grants and moved their families and slaves to settle on and develop the lands received. Some were converted under the preaching of Methodist ministers and wanted to join the church. The same is true of some settlers from Virginia and the Carolinas who could not afford to own slaves but might not be anti-slavery in sentiment.

The opposite would be true of the majority of the migrants entering Kentucky from the northeast via the Ohio River. Few were slaveholders and a majority were strongly abolitionist in belief, and regarded slavery as a moral and social evil.

One can feel confident that preachers appointed to Kentucky would fervently share the abolitionist views of the Methodist Conferences and the General Conferences. The abolition-minded bishops, Francis Asbury and Thomas Coke, could be counted on making their appointments in accordance with the church's position. So we can be assured that all the preachers sent to Kentucky, the presiding elder, Francis Poythress, and the first principal of Bethel Academy, John Metcalf, were not slave-holders at the time of their appointments.

Poythress and Metcalf were from well-to-do families in Virginia and thus were vulnerable to becoming involved with slavery through their family affairs. Neither might they be abolitionist in their views about slavery in regard to their family relationships or with converts who possessed slaves. Though neither man expressed his views in writing, some of the events in their ministry provide some clues.

In Francis Poythress' leadership of the Kentucky Conference, one incident involving his relationship to Rev. Benjamin Ogden may throw some light on his sentiments. Ogden was one of the two young men, the other was James Haw, who were appointed as Methodist missionaries to Kentucky in 1786. They travelled and preached far and wide under the most difficult of circumstances, with success.

In 1787, Rev. Ogden spent most of his time in the Cumberland River watershed and reported sixty-three converts who became Methodists at the end of the year. The next year he married Nancy Puckett, whose family lived near Harrodstown, and moved to Virginia, but returned in 1790 to Kentucky. Because the rule of the church at the time required an evangelist or travelling preacher to give up that kind of ministry when they married, Ogden and his wife located and he preached as opportunities came his way.

There is some mystery concerning what brought about the rift between Ogden and Poythress. J.A. Smith[42] draws from several articles in the *Western Christian Advocate* to propose that Ogden became a spokesman for anti-slavery supporters in the Kentucky Conference who didn't like the views of Poythress and Metcalf regarding slavery. They asked Ogden to preach against slavery at a church service at Bethel Academy, and he did. Smith notes:[43]

"Poythress's administration, according to McHenry, had by then become 'irregular and wild,' and the presiding elder either reproved Odgen 'with great severity,' as Hinde recalled, or 'hurled him out of the church,' as McHenry remembered."

He cites Barnabas McHenry, "Letter to Thomas Hinde, December 7, 1820" published in *Western Christian Advocate* vol. VII, no. 4, p. 1. Friday, May 15, 1840; also Thomas S. Hinde. "Contributions to the Western Historical Society," *Western Christian Advocate*, vol. VII, no. 4, Friday, May 15, 1940.

When Poythress became too ill to function as a minister, he went to the home of his sister, Mrs. Susannah Pryor, who owned a farm in Jessamine County, Kentucky. Very likely he was cared for by some of the many slaves owned by his sister. The will made out by Mrs. Pryor, dated June 1, 1809, contains a bequest of a half share of her 150 acres and six adult slaves and a child to be divided among them, "for their support and maintenance during their natural lives."[44]

Mrs. Pryor died in February 1817 and her will was probated at the March Court in 1817. The appraisement document presented to the court reveals she then owned thirty-two slaves valued at $8,285. Because of his mental break-down, Poythress did not know he had become an owner of several slaves and that they would care for him until he died in 1818.

There is no evidence that John Metcalf possessed slaves while he served the church as principal of Bethel Academy or as pastor of several churches. Neither are there any documents preserved, nor any references made by other Methodist ministers, that indicate Metcalf owned slaves during the last decade of the eighteenth century.

Several of Metcalf's letters to George Nicholas, reproduced earlier in this article, reveal that he had a close legal and personal relationship with that champion of slavery in Kentucky. He respected him enough to push for and obtain from the first officials of Jessamine County the right to name the county seat of the new county, "Nicholasville."

While serving at Bethel Academy, he married a niece of Francis Poythress, Ann (Nancy) Peniston, in 1795. Mrs. Susanna Pryor made a bequest to her of two slaves, Peter and Charlotte and their children. Ann would have gained possession of them in 1817 when her aunt died.

The most revealing information comes from the estate arrangement, dated July 19, 1831, of Rev. John Metcalf who had died in 1820. There were two male slaves and seven women slaves divided among his wife and six children. The two slaves bequeathed to his wife, Ann, were among them. Some or all of the others may have been the children of those two.[45] In regard to John Lewis who gave one hundred acres for Bethel Academy, there were a series of deeds which gave slaves to his daughter-in-law, Nancy, wife of deceased son Thomas, to his living sons, William and Daniel.[46]

Richard Masterson, in whose meeting house the first Kentucky Methodist Conference was held, also became involved in slavery toward the end of his life. He and his wife, Sarah, moved to a farm near Carrolton, Kentucky. W.E. Arnold makes an intriguing statement:[47]

"He farmed on a large scale and owned many slaves. His home again became a center of Methodist influence and a resting place for McKendree and the weary circuit riders. Both he and his wife were deeply religious."

Had the bishop and the circuit riders suddenly become silent about the abolitionist heritage of the Methodist Church, when they entered the Masterson home?

In 1798, Bethel Academy trustee James Hord granted Edwin Hord power to recover slaves for him.[48] A startling illustration of how slavery could entangle the family affairs of a staunch abolitionist is found in the life of the venerable Rev. Valentine Cook. Before he came to Kentucky, he was known as an anti-slavery orator, and when he took over Bethel Academy his position caused him problems. Who he argued with is unclear, but Young's statement about his tenure at Bethel is of interest, "He remained with the school one year. His anti-slavery views induced his removal."[49]

Where did Young obtain this information? I have found no other historian that has said Cook was fired due to his views on slavery. It is possible he got this information from the son of Rev. John Metcalf, Henry, who lived in Nicholasville until his death in 1879.

Cook married Tabitha Slaughter, daughter of a slave owner in 1799. Being converted and a Methodist, she surely had turned her back on slavery, but it involved her and her husband anyway. This fact comes to light in wills they made out before they died.

Cook's will is dated August 12, 1822, shortly before his death.[50] In regard to his wife, he says, "The slaves in my possession came by my wife, Tabitha, they being hers. I leave them (viz) Vincy, Milly and Washington and their issue, if any hereafter, to my wife to be at her own entire disposal forward."

Mrs. Tabitha Cook's will, dated March 26, 1829,[51] contains her bequest of "two negro boys and my negro girl Milly with their issue..." to be divided between her three daughters, Nancy, Eliza, and Susan. The remaining slaves were to be under the control of her oldest son, Richard.

Neither legal document shows any interest in setting the slaves free, in accordance to the earlier laws of the Methodist Episcopal Church. The basic clue to understanding how the early abolitionist stand of these preachers and laymen disappeared and the possession of slaves became acceptable probably resides in the action of 1808 (see above) which transferred decision making about slavery to the annual conferences.

The Western Conference made such a decision in October 1808 also, which reads:[52]

Question: "What method shall be taken with a member of our Society that shall enter into the Slave Trade and shall buy or sell a Slave or Slaves?"

Answer: "Every preacher who has the charge of a circuit shall upon information received cite every such member or members so buying or selling a Slave or Slaves to appear at the ensuing Quarterly Meeting Conference and there to submit his or their case to the judgment of the said Quarterly Meeting Conference who shall proceed to determine whether the Person or Persons have purchased or sold such Slave or Slaves in a case of mercy or humanity or from speculative motives, and if a majority of the Quarterly Meeting Conference judge that they have bought or sold with such speculative motives they shall accordingly expel every such Person or Persons.

"And in case the President of the Quarterly Meeting Conference should differ in judgment from the majority and think they have retained the Person or Persons improperly, he may refer his or their case to the ensuing Annual Conference and if any Person or Persons think they are injured by the decision of the Quarterly Meeting Conference such Person or Persons shall be allowed an appeal to the ensuing Annual Conference, provided they signify the same to the Quarterly Meeting Conference at the time of trial, and the President of the Quarterly Meeting Conference shall cause the minutes of such trial to be laid before the Annual Conference who shall judge and finally determine in every such case."

Francis Asbury, William McKendree
Liberty Hill, Tennessee, October 7th, 1808
William Burke, Secty.

A commentary on this action by Bishop Asbury in his journal has this observation:[53]

We made a regulation respecting slavery; it was, that no member of society, or preacher, should sell or buy a slave unjustly, inhumanly or covetously; the case, on complaint, to be examined for a member by the Quarterly meeting; and for a preacher an appeal to an annual conference; Where the guilt was proved the offender to be expelled.

In accordance with this conference regulation, Jacob Addams was expelled from the Western Conference in 1810, "for purchasing a Negro woman and child with speculative motives,..."[54] Benjamin McReynolds, a local preacher, was refused membership in the conference in 1811, "in Consequence of his not having complied with the rule with regard to a Negro man he holds as a Slave."[55] But in regard to Samuel Sellars who owned a fourteen-year-old male slave, a committee of the conference ruled that he could hold the slave until the boy became twenty-two years old.[56]

A significant feature of the slavery regulation of 1808 and the actions taken in response to the situations of the three men mentioned above is that gaining possession of slaves by inheritance is not mentioned. The concern is limited to dealing with slaves, in the words of Bishop Asbury, "unjustly, inhumanly, or covetously;"[57]

Therefore, it was quite possible for a loyal Methodist lay person or a preacher in the Western Conference to possess slaves after 1808, if they inherited, or gained them within the three limitations mentioned by Bishop Asbury. Consequently, Poythress, Metcalf, Cook, Masterson, Lewis, and others could possess slaves after 1808 and be in accordance with the rules of the Methodist Episcopal Church.

As far as is known, school sessions were not held in the Bethel Academy building, nor did anyone live there until its razing in 1820. There are no explicit statements in the legal documents cited above that the slavery issue caused the demise of Bethel Academy. No person who lived through those events and wrote about them later mentions slavery as the cause, yet the clues outlined above for the period before 1808, seem to support such a conclusion.

After leaving Bethel Academy, Rev. John Metcalf moved his family to a log cabin in the newly created Nicholasville. Here he opened a school for boys, which he soon transferred to a new log building next door. Though Metcalf knew that Rev. Nathaniel Harris was conducting school at Bethel Academy on the banks of the Kentucky River at that time, Metcalf used the same name for his school.

On July 4, 1802, Nicholasville held a community celebration with a parade led by the military, followed by Metcalf's school children and others. Clearly, Metcalf already had his school in operation before this date.[58]

J.A. Smith observes that Metcalf:[59]

> ...went to the Kentucky River site and carted off everything that was not fastened down, presumably to furnish his Nicholasville school. In 1804 the quarterly conference for the Lexington circuit suspended him from the ministry for 12 months for his actions.

W.E. Arnold[60] provides this text of the conference action dated May 19, 1804:

> At a quarterly meeting for Lexington circuit, at J. Griffith's, the members of the Conference were the following: William McKendree, P. E., Learner Blackman, Thomas Wilkerson, Benj. Coleman, Jesse Griffith, David Robertson, Bryan McGrath, Benj. Vanpelt, Nathaniel Harris, William Rutter, Humphrey Lyons, Cornelius Ruddle, Jesse Rowland, Luke Hanson, Elias Johnson, Richard Demit, John Lair.

The case of John Metcalf, L.D., was brought forward from the Committee, who were Jesse Garner, Sl. Newman, Nathaniel Harris.

The charges were as follows, viz., Charge 1st. For removing the property of Bethel Academy without the knowledge or consent of the trustees of Bethel Academy. Charge 2nd. In not giving information of said property, though inquired of in an official manner, 1st, before the Board of Trustees, and 2nd, by one of the Trustees alone. Charge 3rd. For not sending a full account of said property. Charge 4th. In not sending a true account of the time when, (nor by whom), said property was removed. This Conference, taking up the charges one by one, concur in judgment with the above named Committee, and finally give it their judgment, that said J. Metcalf, be reduced to a state of trial, for the time of 12 months, from the present date, and deprived of the liberty of all official services in the Church, for the same term of 12 months.

Signed in behalf of the Conference, By Nathaniel Harris.

Several observations should be noted: 1) In May 1804, the Church, through its quarterly conference, considered itself responsible for what happened at Bethel Academy; 2) John Metcalf was not present at the Conference to defend himself; 3) Evidently, Nathaniel Harris had ceased teaching school at Bethel Academy and had moved out of the building before Metcalf had removed the furniture; 4) the Board of Trustees were still existing as a functioning body, and; 5) Nathaniel Harris probably had taken the lead in bringing charges through the committee to the quarterly conference against Metcalf and he signed the Conference document containing the sanctions against Metcalf.

An action of the 1805 Conference, provides this information: "Samuel Douthit deposited \$20 two years past in the hands of William McKendree, to be appropriated to the paying of a teacher in the Bethel Academy; but failing to employ one, he has refunded the money, by Elisha Bowman."[61]

This action would support the probability that Harris ceased teaching at Bethel in 1803.

Rev. William Burke (Burk) claimed that the Western Conference of 1803 appointed him, "to attend the legislature and obtain an act of incorporation. I performed that duty, and Bethel was incorporated, with all the powers and privileges of a literary institution."[62]

There is a problem here, because the journal of the Western Conference, of which William Burke was secretary, does not contain such an action. Besides, no evidence has been found in the legislative records of Kentucky that Bethel Academy was incorporated at that time. It already had been incorporated by the state February 10, 1798.

The journal of the Western Conference in 1806 does have an action of the Conference concerning Bethel Academy:[63]

The Conference proceeded to raise a fund by Subscription, for the use and benefit of Bethel Academy, in Kentucky.

The Conference proceeded to elect Jacob Young, Samuel Parker, and William

Houston, as trustees of the said fund; whose duty it shall be, to keep regular books, for the purpose of entering Subscriptions, and keeping all the accounts of said fund.

The Conference raised by voluntary subscriptions for the above use, $67.50.

The journal of the Western Conference of 1808 has this action: "The Conference directed that $33.50 now in the hands of the former Trustees of the Charity Fund be deposited with William Burk for the use and benefit of the Trustees of Bethel Academy."[64]

These two conference actions indicate that the Western Conference did not dissociate itself from Bethel Academy in 1804, but continued support of the Trustees of the school beyond 1808. W.W. Sweet preserves the text of the journal of that Conference through 1811 and there is no action to disown Bethel Academy in them.[65]

A legislative act by the General Assembly of Kentucky, dated January 30, 1810, granted permission to Bethel Academy to sell the land granted to it in 1798.[66] In response to this act, Nathaniel Harris and Maddox Fox, trustees of the school, ran this advertisement:[67]

The trustees of Bethel Academy being authorized by the legislature of Kentucky to dispose of their donation LANDS, do offer the following tracts for sale;
2780 acres
On the Ohio River, opposite the mouth of Saline Creek.
1600 acres
In two surveys, adjoining Col. Waggoner's.
755 acres
Adjoining Maj. Fielding Jones. All those lands lie near together, or in separate tracts—several valuable farms on them, a small part of the purchase money will be required in hand, the balance in six annual payments. For further particulars, apply to Nathaniel Harris and Maddox Fisher, in Lexington, Ky.

Did anyone buy any or all of this land? The land in this advertisement totals 5,143 acres of the 6,000 acres granted to Bethel Academy in 1798. What about the remaining 857 acres? Was this tract also sold at some time? That the trustees of Bethel Academy were successful in selling at least some of their land, is suggested by an Act of the General Assembly of Kentucky dated January 26, 1815. This Act authorizes the investment of the proceeds of the sale of seminary lands in bank stock.[68]

The building by the banks of the Kentucky River stood empty until 1820. Several legal documents relate to the disposal of the land and the razing of the building, for removal to Nicholasville, Kentucky.

Surprisingly, in a deed dated June 1, 1816, John Lewis gave the 100 acres on which Bethel Academy was located to his son William.[69] The original deed of 1797 does not have a provision stating that the land reverted to John Lewis, if a school ceased to function in the building on the land. That deed is a quit claim deed with several instances of "forever" in it.[70] Two Acts of the General Assembly of Kentucky suggest that John Lewis was alerted by the trustees of his mistake, for efforts were soon made to obtain authority from the General Assembly to sell the land on which Bethel Academy was located. The first legislative act is dated February 1, 1817, and the second February 6, 1819.[71]

One may surmise that the trustees either verbally returned the land to John Lewis, or failed to record a written deed. A recorded deed, transferring the land back to Lewis, does not exist at the Jessamine County Court House.

On May 24, 1819, John Lewis executed a new deed to his son William, giving him the 100-acre tract of land. On March 22, 1822, John Lewis made another deed, selling the same 100 acres to son William for $1,000. The land descriptions on the several documents are clearly for the same portion of land. William sold the 100 acres on April 19, 1822, to George Walker for $331.[72]

The trustees of Bethel Academy bought lots in Nicholasville, Kentucky. One deed, dated June 12, 1819, transferred two acres from John and Nancy Metcalf to the trustees of Bethel Academy. The cost was $300 paid by Nathaniel Harris, Samuel H. Woodson, William Caldwell, Jesse Head, Thomas B. Scott, John Lewis, James Fletcher and Francis P. Hord.[73]

Two more acres were obtained from Leslie and Margaret Combs on February 24, 1820, costing $200. The trustees who bought the land were: Nathaniel Harris, President, William Caldwell, William Shieve, Francis P. Hord, Robert Crockett, George J. Brown, Archibald Young, and James Fletcher.[74]

These two plots were next to each other, and apparently, soon after these four acres were purchased, the original Bethel Academy was torn down. Brick, lumber, doors, and windows were transported to Nicholasville, Kentucky, and a similar building was constructed, but the size and style is unknown. After the new building was completed, a school for boys was opened. There is no clear evidence that the Methodist Church continued a relationship with Bethel Academy.

At some time after the razing of the original Bethel Academy, some of its bricks and the cornerstone were transferred to Vanderbilt University, Nashville, Tennessee, and incorporated in an outside wall of the engineering building.[75]

John Y. Martin, Teacher of Languages and Professor of General Science, ran this advertisement, April 2, 1821:[76]

> The subscriber informs the public that he continues his school in the Bethel Academy, near the town of Nicholasville, Jessamine County. His next session will commence on the 2nd of April, to continue for five months. Tuition $12.50 per session payable in advance, or $15 payable at the expiration of the session.

The next advertisement related to Bethel Academy was run three years later.[77]

> There is room in the Nicholasville Academy [sic] for a few more pupils. This Academy is now in a prosperous condition. The system of education comprises all that is required for admission into Transylvania University. The course of classical students is full and thorough. The town is perfectly healthy and happily removed from the temptations to be met in larger towns and from the listlessness of a Country residence. Board can be had very low.

Terms of tuition thirty dollars per annum.
James O'Brian, Principal N.A.
References to John Roche, A. M. Transylvania U. Prof.
John Brown, Prin. Prep. Department
Kean O'Hara, A.M. Woodford County

B.H. Young[78] states that A.R. Northrup was principal from 1841-1846, followed by Charles F. Smith. The next extant advertisement is dated May 10, 1848.[79]

On the night of February 13, 1857, tragedy struck Bethel Academy in the form of a destructive fire:[80]

FIRE IN NICHOLASVILLE.—*The Louisville Courier* is informed by correspondence, that a fire broke out, on Friday night about 9 o'clock, in the Venerable building in the back place known as Bethel Academy, and was soon destroyed. At the time of its destruction it was occupied by a prosperous school.

A year later, February 15, 1858, the General Assembly of Kentucky approved an act to amend the act of 1798 to incorporate Bethel Academy.[81] The amendments authorized the election of trustees of Bethel Academy by voters in Jessamine County for terms of six years each. These trustees may elect a president, a treasurer, and a clerk. The trustees were instructed to select and provide tuition for a "beneficiary pupil" from each of the voting precincts. Another Act of the General Assembly, dated February 13, 1864, repealed the action taken February 15, 1858, and directed its attention to the original act of February 10, 1798. The new Act named as "incorporators and trustees of Bethel Academy" the following persons: "George Brown, John S. Bronaugh, Isaac Barkley, Newton Dickerson, Moreau Brown, Lewis H. Chrisman, and Thos. Crutcher." The term of office of these men was to begin July 1, 1864.[82]

A third Act of the General Assembly was approved April 16, 1873, granting the trustees of Bethel Academy to lease or sell its lands to the town of Nicholasville and the proceeds divided among the school districts of the county. [83]

If the trustees actually rented Bethel Academy, they did not do so for long. On July 8, 1876, George Brown, the President ran this advertisement:[84]

The Trustees of Bethel Academy, Nicholasville, Ky., will on Friday, July 14th, 1876, hold an election for a Teacher of this Institution, for the ensuing school year. The names of applicants for the position are solicited, GEO. BROWN, Pres't.

A.N. Gordon was elected as the teacher for that year, and the next year he negotiated a rent agreement with the trustees dated May 28, 1877, which made him principal for ten years.[85] About the same time, the City of Nicholasville constructed Broadway Street which passed through the properties of neighbors south of the Bethel Academy. The trustees of Bethel Academy decided to purchase a fragment of one property that adjoined the property of the school.

This small plot was purchased from S.H. and Carrie Noland on September 24, 1878, for one dollar.[86] The land north of the Academy was purchased from the Jessamine Female Institute on January 27, 1880, for twenty-five dollars.[87]

About five months later a reporter wrote this story:[88]

Nicholasville Items

The Bethany [sic] Academy exercises were very well attended Friday afternoon. The young scholars did honor both to themselves and their teachers. Those who were awarded for their ten months hard study were as follows: Willie Welch received the medal in mathematics. In the Junior class, Master Charles Sparks received a handsome book; in the Junior class Ethelbert Scrogin received five volumes of Macauley's *History of England*, for proficiency in reading: Winn Butler received Worchester's Dictionary for excelling the school in orthography.

The next year, 1881, Gordon ran this advertisement:[89]

Bethel Academy, Nicholasville, Kentucky.

Oldest High School in the State. A full corps of teachers in English, Graphical, Graphimatical and Commercial Courses. Home training. Thorough instructions. Firm discipline. Boys prepared for advanced classes in college or practical business life. Handsome new building. A large, light, and airy school room. A.N. Gordon, Principal.

A few weeks later, an editorial gave this evaluation of Bethel Academy:

Bethel Academy, an advertisement of which appears in this paper is one of the best schools for boys in Kentucky. Prof. A.N. Gordon, the principal, is a graduate of Washington and Lee University, and is one of the finest educators in the land. A new school building has been erected, and the Academy promises to continue in its course of prosperity and usefulness for many years. Parents entrusting their sons to Prof. Gordon's guidance and instruction may be sure that both their mental and moral education will be strictly attended to. Bethel Academy is the oldest High School in the State, and ranks among the very best and most thorough.[90]

In September a duplicate of the July advertisement was printed in the same newspaper.[91] In May 1882, S.M. Duncan published a strongly worded reply to an article, "The School Boy," printed in the newspaper, April 26, 1882.[92] He claimed he had accurate information about the early events and people related to Bethel Academy. However, when his statements are compared with data in this article, several errors become obvious.

During the tenure of A.N. Gordon, several advertisements and brochures were published.[93] One brochure honored the long teaching career of A.N. Gordon and gives the dates of his tenure at Bethel Academy as 1876-1887.[94]

Several types of legal documents are related to Bethel Academy: some are actions of the Board of Councilmen of the town of Nicholasville and some are deeds which transferred property controlled by the trustees of Bethel Academy to other parties.

In the Minutes of July 29, 1893, of the above mentioned Board of Councilmen, are these items of information:[95]

a) A proposition was presented to the Board by the trustees of Bethel Academy offering to sell the Academy campus to the town of Nicholasville to be used as a public school. Reference is made to the failure of the trustees to generate enough tuition fees to pay teachers and thus they had rented the Academy buildings to the town for the past five years (1888-1893).

b) They would sell the land and buildings to the town for seven thousand dollars ($7,000) which, after receiving the money, they would give to the Jessamine Female Institute. The Institute would use this gift to pay off a debt and make improvements on its buildings.

c) The trustees asked for a fifteen hundred dollar down payment in the form of a property trade, namely, the lot and building of public school #1 which lay from the east line of the Academy land to Seminary Street (earlier called Noland Street and later named South Third Street). The remaining five thousand, five hundred dollars were to be paid in three annual installments at six per-cent interest.

d) The trustees asked the Board of Councilmen to set aside one or more rooms in the Academy building for classes designed to prepare students for college. After hearing the proposition from the trustees of Bethel Academy, the Board of Councilmen unanimously voted to accept the offer. A notation was made in the minutes stating that the trustees of Jessamine Female Institute agreed to accept the gift of seven thousand dollars from the trustees of Bethel Academy.

On July 29, 1893, a deed was executed by the trustees of Bethel Academy transferring their land, school building, and a dwelling to the Board of Councilmen.[96] Stipulations mentioned in the proposition presented to the Board of Councilmen on July 25, 1893, are repeated in the deed. No mention is made in the deed about the lot and building of School District #1 being transferred to the trustees as part of the payment plan.

The Minutes of the Board of Councilmen of the town of Nicholasville, dated August 4, 1893,[97] mention that the deed for the property of Bethel Academy had been received and a motion was made to have it recorded at the court house. Another motion empowered a committee to make repairs on Bethel Academy buildings.

The Mayor then told the Board of Councilmen that the trustees of Bethel Academy were requesting that the lot the Board had sold them be deeded to John L. and Emma W. Logan for fifteen hundred dollars.[98] This request and a schedule of payments governing the purchase of the property by the Logans was approved by the Board of Councilmen.

A note of interest here is that for years I was told by long time residents of Nicholasville that the lot and building exchanged between the Board of Councilmen, the trustees of Bethel Academy and the Logans was the original Bethel Academy constructed in 1820-21.

Only recently has research in Court House records revealed that this was not so. This property was only in the possession of the trustees of Bethel Academy from July 29 to August 4, 1893. This research has now made clear that the Bethel Academy land is now the grounds on which the Nicholasville Elementary School is located. The dwelling the Board of Councilmen bought from the trustees has long since disappeared. The Bethel Academy building was probably the old building shown in a 1913 photograph of the early stages of construction of a new High School building. A recently acquired dish has a picture of this old building.

In nearby Wilmore, in 1890, Rev. John Wesley Hughes was planning to start an independent, though Methodist-oriented, school. While praying about a possible name, "Asbury College" came to him. He began reading about Bishop Asbury and discovered he had officially established a school a century earlier about four miles from Wilmore, calling it Bethel Academy. This information confirmed in Hughes' mind the thought that came during his prayer time. He promptly named his new school Asbury College.[99] Seemingly, he was unaware that a Bethel Academy structure was rented at the time by the town of Nicholasville and used for public school purposes. The memory of Bethel Academy impacted the history of Asbury College on December 13, 1925. The President of the college, Dr. Akers, proposed to the Board of Trustees that the High School on campus be renamed Bethel Academy. The trustees agreed to the proposal. A separate building was constructed to house the Academy which was to be self-supporting. This relationship to the college continued until 1938, when the Academy had to be closed. The accreditation standards of the Southern Association of Colleges and Secondary Schools prohibited any connection between the college and the high school.[100]

A renewed interest by the Kentucky Methodist Conference in the original Bethel Academy resulted in the construction of a monument at the site made of stones from the foundation of the school. The Conference had cast a bronze plaque which was attached to the monument. The text on the plaque read thus:

> On this site stood BETHEL ACADEMY, First Church School in all the West Planned by First Methodist Conference in Kentucky, 1790; Opened (about) 1793: closed 1804; Brick building, 40 x 80 feet, three stories high; Stones in this pillar were in original foundation erected by Kentucky Conference Historical Society, 1933.

There are several errors of fact on this plaque: 1) The third line should have read, "First Protestant Church School," because Roman Catholic schools had been built in the West before 1790; 2) The dimensions of the building were 35 x 86 feet. The plaque stayed on the pillar for fifty years but was stolen in 1983 and has never been recovered.

In the spring of 1965, I began excavation at the site. A report of this project is found in another article in this volume.

On March 15, 1984, the original site of Bethel Academy was entered in the National Register of Historic Places. This action gives the school recognition as an important historical, architectural and archaeological site.[101]

The World Methodist Historical Society met at Asbury Theological Seminary August 6-10, 1984. On the afternoon of the tenth, members of the society visited the Bethel Academy site and held a brief service of re-dedication. The founder, Bishop Francis Asbury, and others active in operating and sustaining the academy were honored in a Litany of Re-dedication.[102]

In 1987 the Kentucky Historical Marker Program erected a marker on the Asbury

College campus bordering North Lexington Avenue in Wilmore, Kentucky.[103] On one side is an inscription commemorating the college and on the other side is an inscription with this text:[104]

BETHEL ACADEMY

This was second Methodist school in United States. In 1790 Bishop Francis Asbury laid plans for Bethel Academy, four miles southeast of Wilmore on cliffs above Kentucky River. It was operating by 1794 and closed ca. 1804, due to lack of funds and Indian hostilities. Second site was in Nicholasville, 1820-93.

This author hopes that what is written in this volume commemorating Bethel Academy, will serve as a memorial to the people who raised it up and to this institution that taught young men on the American frontier the Gospel of Jesus Christ.

Notes
1.   J.D. Wright, *Transylvania: Tutor to the West* (1975), pp. 6-11.
2.   Bishop Thomas Coke quoted in "Bethel Academy," *Cyclopedia Of Methodism*, ed. Matthew Simpson (Philadelphia: Louis H. Evarats, 1881), pp. 104-105.
3.   E.T. Clark, *The Journals and Letters of Francis Asbury*, vols. I and II (Nashville: Abingdon Press). See entries for each date.
4.   See copy of this deed in Appendix A, Exhibit 1.
5.   A.W. Cummings, *Early Schools of Methodism* (New York: 1886), p. 50.
6.   B.H. Young, *A History of Jessamine County, Kentucky* (Louisville: Courier-Journal Job Printing Co., 1898), pp. 83-84.
7.   Ibid., p. 172.
8.   Ibid., p. 70.
9.   Ibid., p. 84.
10.   Ibid., p. 71. In the above reproductions of these letters, I have followed the printed format, style, and spelling as closely as possible.
11.   N. Bangs, *A History of the Methodist Episcopal Church* (New York: T. Mason & G. Lane). This is but a portion of the regulations he lists.
12.   See the text of this deed in Appendix A, Exhibit 1.
13.   See the text of this Act in Appendix B, Exhibit 1.
14.   See the text of this Act in Appendix B, Exhibit 2.
15.   A.H. Redford, *The History of Methodism in Kentucky*, vol. 1 (Nashville: Southern Methodist Publishing House, 1870), pp. 124-125.
16.   W.W. Sweet, *The Rise of Methodism in the West* (New York: The Methodist Book Concern, 1920), pp. 93-99.
17.   See the biography of Poythress in the article "Important Men Related to Bethel Academy" in this issue of *The Asbury Theological Journal*.
18.   Thomas Scott, "Letter to the Editors," *Western Christian Advocate* (Cincinnati: April 2, 1841), p. 1. See full text in biography of Francis Poythress. See above.
19.   "A Teacher Wanted," *Kentucky Gazette*, May 23, 1798, p. 1.
20.   Scott, "Letter to the Editors," p. 1.
21.   Young, *History of Jessamine County*, pp. 196-197.
22.   "To the Public," *Kentucky Gazette*, November 28, 1799, p. 1.
23.   See biography of Valentine Cook in the article "Important Men Related to Bethel Academy" in this issue of *The Asbury Theological Journal*.

24. J. Atkinson, *Centennial History of American Methodism*, 1884), pp. 203-204.
25. Redford, *The History of Methodism in Kentucky*, p. 86.
26. W.E. Arnold, *A History of Methodism in Kentucky*, vol. 1 (Louisville: Herald Press, 1935), p. 84.
27. N. Curnock, *The Journal of the Rev. John Wesley*, vol. 5 (London: The Epworth Press, 1938), pp. 445-446.
28. W.T. Smith, *John Wesley and Slavery* (Nashville: Abingdon Press, 1986), pp. 91-96, 121-148.
29. J. Telford, *The Letters of the Rev. John Wesley*, vol. 8 (London: The Epworth Press, 1938), p. 265.
30. In all the quotations from original disciplines, the format, style, syntax, and spelling are preserved as nearly as possible.
31. R. Emory, *History of the Discipline of the Methodist Episcopal Church* (New York: Carlton and Porter, 1856), pp. 14, 15.
32. Ibid., p. 19.
33. Ibid., p. 21.
34. Ibid., pp. 34, 44.
35. "Slavery," *Cyclopedia of Methodism*, p. 805.
36. Ibid.
37. *The Doctrines and Disciplines of the Methodist Episcopal Church in America*, 9th edition (1796), pp. 76-77.
38. Emory, *History of the Discipline,* pp. 329-330.
39. Ibid., pp. 330-331.
40. Ibid., p. 331.
41. W.T. Smith, *John Wesley and Slavery*, pp. 28-29.
42. J.A. Smith, "The Case of Bethel Academy: Methodism's School on the Frontier." *Methodist History*, XXXII, no. 1, 1993, pp. 19-30.
43. Ibid.
44. *Deed Book B* (Jessamine County Court House, Clerk of County Court), pp. 301-303.
45. *Deed Book I* (Jessamine County Court House, Clerk of County Court), pp. 464-465.
46. *Deed Books D,* pp. 473, 474 and *E,* p 114 (Jessamine County Court House, Clerk of County Court).
47. Arnold, *A History of Methodism*, p. 47. An ad in the *Kentucky Gazette*, Nov, 15, 1794, placed by Richard Masterson requests information about a runaway slave named George.
48. *Deed Book 3* (Jessamine County Court House, Clerk of County Court), p. 387.
49. Young, *History of Jessamine County*, p. 173.
50. *Will Book B* (Logan County Court House, Clerk of County Court), p. 196.
51. *Will Book I,* (Logan County Court House, Clerk of County Court), p. 185.
52. Sweet, *The Rise of Methodism*, p. 148, 151.
53. Ibid., p. 151.
54. Ibid., p. 184.
55. Ibid., p. 194.
56. Ibid., p. 203.
57. Ibid., p. 151.
58. Young, *History of Jessamine County*, pp. 100-103.
59. J.A. Smith, "The Case of Bethel Academy," p. 30.
60. Arnold, *History of Methodism*, p. 123.
61. Sweet, *The Rise of Methodism*, p. 105.
62. Quoted by James A. Finley, *Sketches of Western Methodism* (Cincinnati: The Methodist Book Concern, 1857), p. 43.

63. Sweet, *The Rise of Methodism*, pp. 119-120.
64. Ibid., p. 150.
65. Ibid., pp. 73-207.
66. See text of this Act in Appendix B, Exhibit 3.
67. *Kentucky Gazette*, May 7, 1811, p. 2.
68. See the text of this Act in Appendix B, Exhibit 4.
69. See the text of this deed in Appendix A, Exhibit 2.
70. See the text of this original deed in Appendix A, Exhibit 1.
71. See the texts of these two Acts in Appendix B, Exhibits 5 & 6.
72. *Deed Book D* (Jessamine County Court House, Clerk of Court), pp. 422-423; also *Deed Book F*, p. 90; *Deed Book G*, pp. 207, 225-226. See the text of these deeds in Appendix A.
73. *Deed Book F* (Jessamine County Court House, Clerk of Court), p. 104.
74. Ibid., p. 219.
75. E.T. Clark, *An Album of Methodist History* (Nashville: Abingdon-Cokesbury Press, 1952), p. 287.
76. "Advertisement," *Kentucky Reporter*, Lexington, Ky., April 2, 1821, p. 3.
77. "Advertisement," *The Lexington Public Advertiser*, Lexington, Ky., July 15, 1824, p. 4.
78. Young, *History of Jessamine County*, p. 175.
79. See text of this advertisement in Appendix C, Exhibit 2.
80. "Fire in Nicholasville," Appendix C, Exhibit 2, February 18, 1857, p. 3.
81. See the text of this Act in Appendix B, Exhibit 7.
82. See the text of this Act in Appendix B, Exhibit 8.
83. See the text of this Act in Appendix B, Exhibit 9.
84. *Kentucky Gazette*, July 8, 1876, p. 1.
85. See the text of this agreement in Appendix A, Exhibit 8.
86. See the text of this deed in Appendix A, Exhibit 9.
87. See the text of this deed in Appendix A, Exhibit 10.
88. *Lexington Weekly Press*, June 9, 1880, p. 8.
89. *The Lexington Daily Transcript*, July 21, 1881, p. 1. B.H. Young states that "the buildings," were erected in 1878 for $7,000. Young, *History of Jessamine County*, p. 175.
90. *The Lexington Daily Transcript.*, August 8, 1881, p. 1.
91. Ibid., September 6, 1881, p. 2.
92. See text of this article in Appendix C, Exhibit 3.
93. See the texts of these advertisements and brochures in Appendix C, Exhibits 4, 5, 6, and 7.
94. See brochure honoring A.N. Gordon's years of service as a teacher in Appendix C, Exhibit 8. This brochure lists Gordon's tenure at Bethel Academy as 1876 to 1887.
95. See text of these Minutes in Appendix A, Exhibit 11.
96. See text of this deed in Appendix A, Exhibit 12.
97. See text of these Minutes in Appendix, Exhibit 13.
98. See text of this deed in Appendix A, Exhibit 14.
99. J.A. Thacker Jr., *Asbury College: Vision and Miracle* (Nappanee, IL: Evangel Press, 1990), pp. 19-20.
100. Ibid., pp. 133-134.
101. "Remote 160-year Ruins of Southwest Jessamine County Boys School in Spotlight," *The Jessamine Journal*, April 26, 1984, p.1.
102. See text of this Litany of Re-dedication in Appendix C, Exhibit 9.
103. See text of this brochure in Appendix C, Exhibit 10.
104. "Asbury Historical Marker Unveiled Friday Morning," *The Jessamine Journal*, October 13, 1988.

CHAPTER 3:
IMPORTANT MEN RELATED
TO BETHEL ACADEMY

G. HERBERT LIVINGSTON

In the article, "The Bethel Academy Story," reference was made to a number of people who joined their lives and dedicated their labor to build and operate Bethel Academy. Among these people were an inner core who envisioned and brought to reality this frontier school for boys.

This article is a series of short biographies of several men. The first one is the famous Methodist bishop, Francis Asbury. Apart from the affairs of Bethel Academy, the others: Rev. Francis Poythress, Rev. John Metcalf, Rev. Valentine Cook, Rev. Nathaniel Harris, and laymen Richard Masterson and John Lewis, are little known. The life of each person will be briefly summarized and evaluated in terms of their input on the affairs of Bethel Academy.

BISHOP FRANCIS ASBURY

Since many articles and books have been written about the life and work of Bishop Asbury, this biography will be limited to basic data found in *The Journals and Letters of Francis Asbury*, vol. I, edited by E.T. Clark, and that relate to Bethel Academy.

Francis was born in Handsworth Parish, Staffordshire, England. His parents were Joseph and Elizabeth Asbury. According to the calendar of his childhood, the Julian Calendar, Francis was born December 30, 1745.[1]

The Gregorian Calender was adopted in 1752 in Great Britain and the American Colonies and by its calculations Francis was born August 20, 1745, a date most frequently found in his biographies.

Because of many beatings from a cruel, male teacher, Francis dropped out of school at age thirteen. He was converted at age fourteen and began preaching at age sixteen, though he was not licensed to preach until he was eighteen. He served under John Wesley for four years, in charge of a series of circuits. At a conference in Bristol, August 17, 1771, Francis heard John Wesley's plea for preachers to go to America. He volunteered for service and arrived in Philadelphia October 27, 1771.

After several months of riding from place to place holding services, Francis received a letter from John Wesley stating he was appointed as the superintendent of the various Methodist societies springing up in the cities of New York, Philadelphia, Baltimore, and nearby towns. During the Revolutionary War he had to live in hiding for two years, because of his ties to Methodism in England, and his refusal to pledge allegiance to the American colonies. He gradually convinced the colonists he was their friend, and more and more preached in Methodist churches.

John Wesley finally decided to ordain Dr. Thomas Coke as a superintendent of Methodist churches in America and sent him to America to ordain Francis Asbury. Francis insisted on being elected to the office by the American Methodist ministers. At the Christmas Conference held in Baltimore from December 24, 1784 to January 3, 1785, Asbury was elected superintendent, but since he was a layman, Dr. Coke ordained Francis a deacon on Christmas day, an elder the next day and on the 27th, he ordained Francis a superintendent, a term soon changed to bishop. At the same conference those present organized themselves as the Methodist Episcopal Church.

As mentioned in a previous article, "The Bethel Academy Story," Bishop Asbury came to Kentucky by horseback in May 1790 and held the first Methodist conference at Masterson's Station May 13-16 near present day Lexington, Kentucky. Entries in his journal that relate to his first trip to Kentucky, the establishment of Bethel Academy, and its early period of giving instruction to pioneer boys, are reproduced here:

April, 1790
Wednesday, 7...Now it is that we must prepare for danger, in going through the wilderness. I received a faithful letter from brother Poythress in Kentucky, encouraging me to come. This letter I think is well deserving of publication....

Friday, 9...Thence we went on to brother Gott's, and to brother P——'s; and thence, groping through the woods, brother Easley's; depending on the fidelity of the Kentucky people, hastening them, and being unwilling they should wait a moment for me....

May, 1790
Monday, 3...Sabbath night, I dreamed the guard from Kentucky came for me; and mentioned it to brother Whatcoat. In the morning I retired to a small stream, for meditation and prayer, and whilst there saw two men come over the hills: I felt a presumption that they were the Kentucky men, and so they proved to be; they were Peter Massie and John Clark, who were coming for me, with the intelligence that they had left eight men below: after reading the letters and asking counsel of God, I consented to go with them.

Friday, 7...We formed the whole of our company at the Valley Station; besides brother Whatcoat and myself, we were sixteen men....

Thursday, 13...Our conference was held at brother Masterson's, a very comfortable house and kind people. We went through our business in great love and harmony. I ordained Wilson Lee, Thomas Williamson, and Barnabas M'Henry, elders. We had preaching noon and night, and souls were converted, and the fallen restored. My soul has been blessed among these people, and I am exceedingly pleased with them. I would not, for the worth of all the place, have been prevented in this visit, having no doubt but that it will be for the good of the present rising generation. It is true, such exertions of mind and body are trying; but I am supported under it; if souls are saved, it is enough. Brother Poythress is much alive to God. We fixed a plan for a school, and called it Bethel; and obtained a subscription of upwards of three hundred pounds, in land and money, towards its establishment.

Monday, 17...Rode to Coleman's chapel, about ten miles from Lexington, and preached to an unengaged people. We thence rode to John Lewis's, on the bend of Kentucky River. Lewis is an old acquaintance, from Leesburg, Virginia; I was pleased to find that heaven and religion was not lost sight of in his family. Brother Lewis offered me one hundred acres of land for Bethel, on a good spot for building materials.

April, 1792
Wednesday, 11...I wrote an address on behalf of Bethel school. The weather was wet, and stopped us until Friday.

Monday, 23...I rode to Bethel. I found it necessary to change the plan of the house, to make it more comfortable to the scholars in cold weather. I am too much in company, and hear so much about Indians, convention, treaty, killing and scalping, that my attention is drawn more to these things than I would wish. I found it good to get alone in the woods and converse with God.

April 1793
Tuesday, 23...I was at Bethel—the place intended for a school.

Tuesday, 30...Wednesday, May 1, Thursday, 2. We spent in conference; and in openly speaking our minds to each other. We ended under the melting, praying, praising power of God. We appointed trustees for the school; and made sundry regulations relative thereto: we read the Form of Discipline through, section by section, in conference.

Saturday, 4...Came to Bethel to meet the trustees.

Sunday, 5...We had an awful time whilst I opened and applied, "Knowing therefore the terror of the Lord, we persuade men." It was a feeling, melting time, among old and young; and I am persuaded good was certainly done this day. I feel a good deal tired in spirit, yet, blessed be God, I still have peace within; God is all to me: I want more faith to trust him with my life, and all I have and am.

October, 1800.
Saturday, 4...I came to Bethel. Bishop Whatcoat and William M'Kendree preached: I was so dejected I could say little; but weep. Sabbath day it rained, and I kept at home. Here is Bethel; Cokesbury in miniature, eighty by thirty feet,

three stories, with a high roof, and finished below. Now we want a fund of three hundred per year to carry it on; without which it is useless. But it is too distant from public places; its being surrounded by the river Kentucky in part. We now find it to be no benefit: thus all our excellencies are turned into defects. Perhaps brother Poythress and myself were as much overseen with this place as Dr. Coke was with the seat of Cokesbury. But all is right that works right, and all is wrong that works wrong, and must be blamed by men of slender sense for consequences impossible to foresee—for other people's misconduct. Sabbath day, Monday and Tuesday, we were shut up in Bethel with the travelling and local ministry and the trustees that could be called together. We ordained fourteen or fifteen local and travelling deacons. It was thought expedient to carry the first design of education into execution, and that we should employ a man of sterling qualifications, to be chosen by and under the direction of a select number of trustees and others, who should obligate themselves to see him paid, and take the profits, if any, arising from the establishment. Dr. Jennings was thought of, talked of, and written to. I visited John Lewis, who lately had his leg broken; I left him with good resolutions to take care of his soul.

Friday, 10…We rode to Pleasant Run to John Springer's: it was a very warm day for the season. I had a running blister on my side, yet I rode and walked thirty-two miles. We refreshed ourselves at Crawford's Tavern upon the way. We have visited Knox, Madison, Mercer, and Washington counties in this state. It was strongly insisted upon that I should say something before I left Bethel; able or unable, willing or unwilling: accordingly, on Tuesday, in the academical hall, I gave a long, temperate talk upon Heb. x, 38, 39.

Though Bishop Asbury came to Kentucky repeatedly after the above date and stopped in Fayette and Jessamine Counties to preach and visit friends, he never mentions another visit to the site of Bethel Academy in his journal.

Bishop Asbury never married; he left the girl he was dating, Nancy Brookes, behind in England. During a ministry of forty-five years in America, he travelled more than a quarter of a million miles in carriage and on horseback, held numerous conferences and preached over 16,000 sermons. Each year he moved from the northeast to South Carolina, then west over the mountains to the frontier churches, then back through Pennsylvania and New York. He crossed the Appalachian Mountains sixty times. He died in the humble home of a Methodist layman March 31, 1816, near Fredericksburg, Virginia. He was buried by the house but his remains were finally placed in Mt. Olivet Cemetery in Baltimore, Maryland, in 1854.

FRANCIS POYTHRESS

Francis Poythress was born in Virginia of well-to-do plantation owners. *The Virginia Historical Index* lists a column and a half of Poythress names. There are thirty-seven references for the name "Francis."[2]

The earliest biography of this minister of the Gospel, and the basis for most information about him, is an article by Judge Thomas Scott.[3] Since it is not easily accessible, it is reproduced here as it was printed:

Messrs. Elliott and Hamline,—The name of thee Rev. Francis Poythress having been recently been brought before the public with reference to the afflictive malady by which the Church was deprived of a useful minister, we ask liberty, through the medium of the *Western Christian Advocate*, to communicate a few facts illustrative of his character and sufferings:

Our acquaintance with him commenced in April 1794, and continued without much interruption for about six years, during which period we learned from him the following particulars: On the death of his father he inherited a handsome personal and real estate; and being, in early life, thus left, without any one to control his actions, he yielded to the impulses of his passions, which were violent, and rushed into all the follies and vices of youth. The circumstance which brought him to review his past life, was, the reproof of a lady of elevated standing in society. Her reproof carried conviction to his heart. He left her house in confusion, and on his way home resolved to amend his ways. He commenced reading the Scriptures and praying in secret—soon saw and felt the exceeding sinfulness of sin, groaned to be released from its galling chain. That led him to inquire after those persons whom he supposed capable of instructing him in the right way; but for a long time he sought in vain. At length he heard of the Rev. Deveraur Janet [*sic.* correct spelling, Deveraux Jarratt] an Episcopalian clergyman of learning and deep piety, then residing in a remote part of Virginia, whom he visited, and with whom he remained a considerable time, hearing and receiving instruction. Having at length obtained redemption in the blood of Jesus, he soon became sensible of his call to the ministry. He conferred not with flesh and blood, but immediately commenced his itinerant career, preaching the Gospel of the grace of God to all who would hear. This was prior to the time in which our Methodist preachers reached that part of Virginia in which he lived.

On one of his preaching excursions through the southern parts of Virginia and North Carolina, he fell in with one of our traveling preachers (whose name we have forgotten), with whom he formed an acquaintance, who furnished him with the Doctrines and Discipline of our Church, as drawn up by Mr. Wesley. These he read and attentively considered, and being convinced they were based on the Scriptures of divine revelation, he applied for admission, and was received into union and fellowship in the Church.

The Minutes of the several annual conferences show all the circuits he traveled, except one, and districts over which he presided. They are as follows: 1776, Carolina. We are unable to name the circuit he traveled the following year; but from the facts that in 1778 he was received into full connection, and appointed to the charge of Hanover circuit, we infer, that he traveled some circuit in 1777. In 1779, Sussex; 1780, New Hope; 1781, Fairfax; 1782, Talbot; and 1783, Alleghany. In that year, we believe, he extended his ministerial labors across the Alleghany Mountains on to the waters of the Little Youghioghany. In 1784, Colvert; and 1785 Baltimore. In 1786, he was ordained an elder in the

Church, and presided over the district composed of Brunswick, Sussex, and Amelia circuits. From the fact that in 1786 he was ordained an elder, we infer, that in 1785 he was ordained a deacon; and if so, he was among the first of our American preachers who were ordained to that office. In 1787, he presided over the district composed of the circuits of Guilford, Halifax, New Hope, and Caswell, and in 1788 he was transferred to Kentucky; and, in conjunction with Rev. James Haw, appointed to preside over the two former of these circuits. In 1790, Haw's functions as presiding elder ceased, and Poythress presided over the entire district. In 1790, Madison and Limestone circuits were formed, and added to his district. In 1791, the circuits south of the Kentucky River were reformed, the name of Madison being dropped, and that of Salt River substituted; and brother Poythress continued to preside over his district; In 1792, the following (1) circuits were added to his district; Greenbrier, Cowpasture, Bottetourt, and Bedford. In 1793, the four circuits last named were taken from his district, but Hinkstone circuit, then formed, was added to it. There were no other changes made in the bounds of his district during the years 1794, 1795, 1796, except that this last named year, Shelby circuit was formed, and, together with Logan and Guilford, added to it. (2) In 1797, Shelby circuit was dropped, and the Rev. John Kobler, was appointed presiding elder, and the Rev. Francis Poythress, supernumerary, over the district. In the fall of that year, brother Kobler crossed over on to the northwest side of the Ohio River, and formed the Miami circuit, and brother Poythress resumed his station on the district, over which he continued to preside until the end of that year. In 1798, the Rev. Francis Poythress and Jonathan Bird were appointed presiding elders of the district composed of New River, Russell, Holston, and Green circuits, and Rev. Valentine Cook was appointed presiding elder over the Kentucky district. Shortly after brother Cook's arrival in Kentucky (and we feel quite sure it was before he had completed one round on his district), he received instructions from Bishop Asbury to take charge of Bethel Academy, then on the decline for want of a suitable teacher, and brother Poythress was instructed to take charge of the district. Cook therefore took charge of the academy; Poythress of the district, and Bird remained on the station to which he had been appointed. In 1799, New River, Holstone, and Russell, Green and Miami circuits were added to the Kentucky district, and brother Poythress was appointed presiding elder over it. Late in the fall of that year, his bodily and mental powers gave way and fell into ruins. In 1800, he was, however, appointed presiding elder of the district composed of Morganton and Swanino, Yadkin, Salisbury, Haw-River, Guilford, Franklin, Caswell, Tar-River, Newbern, Goshen, Wilmington, Contentney, Pandico, Roan-Oak, Mattamuskeet and Banks; but his affliction rendered it impracticable for him to take the station assigned him.

Upon inspecting the bound Minutes, p. 245, it will be seen, that the Rev. William M'Kendree was, in that year, appointed presiding elder of the district, composed of Greenbrier, Bottetourt, Bedford, Orange, Amherst, Williamsburg and Hanover, and Gloucester circuits, and no presiding elder is named for the

Kentucky district. So soon as Bishop Asbury received information of the malady under which brother Poythress was suffering, he gave instructions to brother M'Kendree to proceed to Kentucky, and take charge of the district; and about the latter end of the summer of that year brother M'Kendree came on the district. In 1802 and 1803, the name of brother Poythress stands recorded in the Minutes among the elders, but without any station being assigned him; after which we anxiously sought for his name, but it was not there. We have heard that he died many years since, but when and how he died we are uninformed.

Bishop Asbury visited Kentucky for the first time in 1790, after which he never visited that state (if we rightly remember), until subsequent to the year 1800; and during these periods, brother Poythress presided over each annual conference which sat in Kentucky, and the stationing of the preachers, and government of the societies within his district, were almost exclusively confided to him by the Bishop.

Bishop Asbury was an excellent judge of men. He was intimately acquainted with brother Poythress; and the stations to which he appointed him, furnishes conclusive evidence of the estimate he set upon him as a man, and Christian minister.

Brother Poythress was grave in his deportment, and chaste in his conversation, constant in his private devotions, and faithful in the discharge of his ministerial duties. We have no recollection of his having ever disappointed a congregation, unless prevented by sickness or disease. As often as practicable, he visited from house to house, instructed and prayed in the family. Among the preachers, he, like most other men, may have had his particular favorites, but all were treated by him with due benevolence and Christian respect. He was unwearied in his efforts to unite the travelling and local ministry as a band of brothers, so that their united efforts might be exerted in furthering the cause of God.

As the weight of all the Churches in his district rested upon him, he sensibly felt the responsibility of his station, and put forth his utmost efforts to discharge, with fidelity, these important trusts which had been confided in him. The education of the rising generation he dreamed to be intimately connected with the interests of the Church, and the result of that conviction was the erection of Bethel Academy. The erection of that institution, we are quite certain, met the approbation of Mr. Asbury, and a majority of the traveling and local preachers of that day.

The conversational powers of brother Poythress were not of a high order, yet when he did engage in general conversation, he maintained his part with propriety, evincive of an extensive knowledge of men and things. His rank as a preacher was not above mediocrity. He was, however, sound in his faith, in doctrine, in purity. There are many words in common use, which he could not pronounce correctly; this we attributed to his loss of teeth.

He was (if we rightly remember), about five feet eight or nine inches in height, and heavily built. His muscles were large, and in the prime of life, we presume, he was a man of more than ordinary muscular strength. He dressed plain and neat. When we first saw him, we supposed, he had passed his 60th year. His muscles were quite flacid, eyes sunken in his head, hair gray (turned back, hanging down on his shoulders), complexion dark, and countenance grave, inclining to melancholy. His step was, however, firm, and general appearance such as to command the respectful consideration of others. He possessed high, honorable feelings, and a deep sense of moral obligation. In general, he was an excellent disciplinarian. He endeavored to probe to the bottom of each wound in the Church, in order that a radical cure might be effected; but would never consent to expel from the bosom of the Church those who evidenced contrition and amendment. And when free from the morbid action of his system, to which it becomes our painful duty to refer, we esteemed him to be a man of sound discriminating judgment. We, however, claim not for him exemption from error, the common frailty of man, and therefore concede to our excellent friend Daviess, of Kentucky, that he may have inflicted a wound on the character of Rev. Benjamin Ogden. But we cannot concede it as a fact, that brother Poythress was influenced in his conduct, by an impure or wicked motive. We were too long and intimately acquainted with him to harbor, for one moment, an idea so uncharitable, and derogatory to his Christian character.

We never had the pleasure of a personal acquaintance with brother Ogden, but having heard him preach his last sermon east of the Mountains, in 1786, when on his journey, as a missionary to Kentucky, we read, with great satisfaction, Mr. Daviess' vindication of his character. We, however, thought there were in that vindication, some expressions a little too harsh, and calculated to lead others to an erroneous conclusion respecting the character of brother Poythress.

Symptoms of insanity, were, at times, discoverable in brother Poythress several years prior to the time he ceased to travel and to preach, and such may have been his situation at the time the unpleasant circumstance occurred, to which brother Daviess refers. We, therefore, put to him to say, whether the vail of Christian charity ought to be drawn over actions induced by a morbid excitement of the system, materially affecting, at the time, his intellectual faculties.

During the latter part of the summer, fall, and winter of 1794 and 1795, brother Poythress, at times, exhibited the appearance of a man whose mind was drawn off from surrounding objects, and in that situation he would sometimes remain for one or more hours, when his system appeared to react, and he would engage in conversation as usual. At other times he complained of giddiness and pains in his head, and his stomach and bowels appeared to be affected with flatulency and acrid eructations. A general listlessness, irksomeness, and disgust seemed to overwhelm him. His countenance appeared sad and sullen, and he evinced an utter aversion and inability to engage in business of importance. At such times, he usually betook himself to bed, but did not appear to sleep soundly. These symptoms became more frequent during the fore part of the year 1795, and would sometimes last for hours. Near the close of the summer of 1795, Rev. Aquila Sugg, who traveled the Lexington circuit, in consequence of bad health, was rendered incapable of performing effective service; and at the request of brother Poythress, we took charge of the circuit until the ensuing spring. Our first quarterly meeting was held in a small log meeting-house not far from Versailles, Woodford county. On Saturday, brother Poythress arrived just before the time of commencing the public exercises—complained of being exceeding unwell, and went to bed. In a few minutes he called, and said, "Brother Scott, you must conduct the quarterly meeting, I can take no part in the public exercises." On returning from meeting, we found him still in bed, but finally prevailed on him to get up. We then walked out together, but had not proceeded far out of the hearing of others, when he suddenly stopped, and said, "Brother Scott, I am a ruined man, a conspiracy has been formed against me by my sister Prior, Mr. Willis Green, and brother Simon Adams. My sister Prior charges me with having kept back part of the price of some negroes I sold for her several years since; Mr. Willis Green accuses me with having embezzled part of the money I collected for Bethel Academy, and brother Adams accuses me with having taken advantage of him in the purchase of a horse; the officers of justice are now in pursuit of me. I shall soon be incarcerated in prison, my character be ruined, and the Church disgraced." I assured him, I knew each of those individuals to be his fast, adhering friends, and incapable of harboring a suspicion injurious to his character, and that he might rest assured they had not formed a conspiracy against him. But all I said had no effect, and he pertinaciously insisted that what he said was true, and said, "they were then engaged in drawing others into their conspiracy." During that conversation, his countenance exhibited a ghastly appearance, and his whole frame trembled. On returning to the house, he again retired to bed, where he remained (if we rightly remember), with his head generally covered, until the next Monday morning, when he was again prevailed on to get out of bed. After he had taken some refreshments, we again walked out together, and I urged him to return home to his sister's, assured him no conspiracy had been formed against him and that if all he imagined were true, it was far better for him promptly to meet the danger, than to attempt to flee from it like a coward.

That advice seemed to strike the right chord, it immediately vibrated, and after a few minutes, he answered, "It is perhaps best promptly to meet the danger, but I cannot do so, unless you will attend and conduct the quarterly meeting for me at Browder's meeting house, near Bardstown, on next Saturday and Sunday. That meeting must not be neglected." We promised to comply with his request, and he returned to his sister's. That was the first clear and unequivocal evidence of partial insanity, which we recollect of having noticed in brother Poythress—insanity as it respected three most intimate friends; for the conspiracy, and the causes leading to it, which he supposed to exist, had no existence, except in his own heated imagination, and, for the time being, it was found to be impracticable to remove those delusive ideas from his mind.

We were confident no conspiracy had been formed against him, as he imagined, and still we entertained fears that in the particular cases named, he had yielded to the temptations of the arch enemy of souls; and that a conviction of his crimes, and fear of detection, had produced the effects we witnessed. Having, however, since that time, acquired some little knowledge of the symptoms which often exhibit themselves in partial insanity, the fears we then entertained have entirely vanished. We mention this, in order to show, how extremely careful we ought to be, not to suffer suspicions deleterious to the character of another to make a lodgement in our minds.

Agreeably to promise, we attended the quarterly meeting, and in meeting brother Poythress, he exclaimed, "Why, upon earth, don't you suffer me to leave you? It was all a delusion. My sister met me as usual." Even in the year 1797, he was confined by affliction, but whether his mind was affected during that affliction, we are entirely uninformed. The last time we saw him was in the fore part of the winter of 1800. The balance of his mind was lost, and his body lay a complete wreck. His labors in the Church militant were at an end, but the fruits of his labors still remain.

We are not aware that any hereditary trait existed, which, in its ultimate range, dethroned his reason; but we can readily imagine that the seeds of that dreadful malady were sown in his system, but the constant exposures and sufferings during the war of the Revolution, and for twelve years he traveled and preached in the then almost wilderness of the west. Among the eight pioneers of Methodism in Kentucky and Tennessee in the year 1788, the name of Francis Poythress, stands pre-eminently with those intrepid heroes of the cross, the foundation of Methodism was laid in those states in which others have since built, and others are now building. Their names ought to be held in grateful remembrance by all who love the Lord Jesus Christ in sincerity and truth. And among all, we are inclined to the opinion, he is not one of them to whom the members of our Church, in those states, owe a greater debt of gratitude, than to Francis Poythress.

Yours in the bonds of a peaceful Gospel.
Thomas Scott
Chillicothe, O., December 11, 1840

A few observations may be added to the data contained in this article by Scott. While Bethel Academy was being built and then operated as a school, Rev. Poythress served as president of the trustees appointed by Bishop Asbury.

Scott admits to lack of knowledge of Poythress' relationship to the church after he became ill. The journal of the Western Annual Conference of 1802 has these notations:[4]

The Conference proceeded to take into Consideration the critical, deranged state of unaccountability which Francis Poythress at present is in, and judge it best, for the safety of the Connection, that his name shall be left off the General Minutes. But at the same time we are tenderly concerned for his support and welfare,—and therefore Resolve, That his name shall stand in our Journal; and that he shall have a proportionable Claim on the Western Conference for his support; and further it is our opinion, that his name should be perpetuated on the Journals of the Conference, for the same purpose.

The report of the Committee of Claims shows in the same minutes a sum of twenty dollars granted to Francis Poythress. Also a notation: "It appears to this Committee, that William McKendree has, in the course of this year, paid Francis Poythress's acct., $13.69, and beged, and applied, $11 more, to the same purpose"[5]

The journal of the same conference of 1803 has this notation:[6]

"Francis Poythress stands on our Journal as a claiment for $80.00. But it appears that he is able to support himself, and does not expect or wish his support from us. We therefore judge, he should not be considered as dependent on us."

The reason Poythress was able to support himself rested on the kindness of his sister Mrs. Susanna Pryor who had a large farm and many slaves in Jessamine County, Kentucky. She took him into her home and placed him under the care of her slaves, several of whom she bequeathed to him so he could be cared for after she died in 1817. Francis lived for another year.

Bishop Asbury visited Poythress in 1810 while traveling through Kentucky. His entry dated Monday, October 15, is short and poignant: "This has been an awful day to me. I visited Francis Poythress, if thou be he; but O how fallen!" The total mental collapse of his friend was almost more than he could bear.[7]

JOHN METCALF

In the article "The Bethel Academy Story," Rev. John Metcalf was discussed quite often. This brief biography will summarize some information not found there, and tie the data in the article together in a sequence.

John Metcalf was born in Southhampton County, Virginia, in 1758 to a well-known family. *The Virginia Historical Index*[8] has a number of entries under the Metcalf and Metcalfe names. His father was Henry.[9] Nothing is known about how he became acquainted with Methodist preachers, nor how and when he was converted. Records of the early years of the Methodist Episcopal Church[10] do not show John Metcalf as received on trial as a preacher in 1790, but he is listed as assigned to the Cumberland, Virginia, circuit with John Lindsey. The minutes of 1791 show that he was continued on trial that year, so his name must have been omitted in 1790 accidentally. That year he was appointed to the Banks circuit in Virginia. He was ordained a deacon and appointed to the Bedford, Virginia, circuit and to the Bottetourt, Virginia, circuit in 1793.

In 1794 he was sent to be co-pastor of the Lexington, Kentucky, circuit with Tobias Gibson. Metcalf had a dual task that year—he was also designated the principal of Bethel Academy which he opened for instruction either in January or June, depending on the accuracy of the dates on the three versions of a letter he sent to George Nicholas.[11] See the text of these letters in the article, "The Bethel Academy Story." Since the 1794 conference met on April 15, of that year, this fact may indicate the June date is correct.

While in charge of Bethel Academy, Metcalf married in 1795 a niece of his presiding elder, Rev. Francis Poythress. She was Ann (Nancy), daughter of Thomas and Elizabeth (Poythress) Peniston, who lived near Lexington, Kentucky. Together they managed Bethel Academy until 1798. That same year they built a log home among a small cluster of log structures about ten miles to the northeast. Anticipating that a portion of Fayette County would soon become Jessamine County, Metcalf, having surveying skills, laid out several streets. Soon the place was called Nicholasville and made the county seat. Metcalf was successful in his efforts to honor his friend George Nicholas in this way.[12]

In the year these events took place, 1799, Metcalf founded a Methodist society in Nicholasville and promoted the construction of a building for the congregation. This is interesting, because in 1795, Metcalf was located and thus not appointed to a circuit in official records of the Methodist Episcopal Church.[13] Neither is the Nicholasville congregation mentioned in the early Journals of the Western Conference from 1800 through 1811.[14]

Either in the fall of 1801 or early in 1802, Metcalf started a school for boys in his home and then in a log structure next door. He called it Bethel Academy, though Rev. Nathaniel Harris was still conducting classes at the original site by the Kentucky River. When Harris closed the school, Metcalf took all moveable equipment from the original building and used it for his own purposes. For this act he was suspended from ministerial activity for twelve months.[15] Metcalf continued his school in Nicholasville for over a decade and a half, but also engaged in the ministerial activities of preaching and marrying couples. At the same time he served as a Justice of Peace from at least 1804 to 1812. He also was much involved in the buying and selling of real estate in Jessamine County, as a series of deeds recorded in the county court house indicate.

In 1818, Metcalf began selling some of his property. A two-acre plot was sold to the trustees of Bethel Academy for a new building to be constructed from materials gained from razing the original structure in 1820.

Apparently, Metcalf closed his Bethel Academy about this time and did not live to see the new Bethel Academy completed. He died August 15, 1820, at the age of sixty-two. He was survived by his wife, Ann, and five children: Henry, b. Nov. 9, 1800; Elizabeth, b. Feb. 23, 1805; Sarah; John W.; and Lucy Ann. Cemetery gravestones show two children died before their father: Lucy A. age 19 years, d. July 26, 1815, and Thomas H, age fifteen, d. Jan 21, 1815.[16] His estate was settled July 19, 1832.[17]

VALENTINE COOK

The contact of Rev. Valentine Cook with Bethel Academy was brief, but it occurred at a crucial period in the existence of the original Bethel Academy, the years 1798 to 1880. A summarized biography of his life and ministry should be enlightening.

Valentine Cook, fifth son of Valentine Sr. and Susannah Baughman, was born in 1765 in York County, Pennsylvania. When he was a child, his parents moved to Greenbrier County, Virginia (now West Virginia). He had limited formal education, but he read every book he could find and studied English grammar carefully. He had a special interest in the Bible and read it often, memorizing many portions of it.

During his youth, he heard a Methodist preacher and was converted. His family at first was cool to this new religious fervor, but before long they were persuaded by their son to start family devotions. His parents were soon converted.

His father sent him to Cokesbury College, the first Methodist school in America, and Valentine Jr. soon became known as that school's brightest student. He became proficient in Latin and Greek and could speak German fluently.

After completing his studies at Cokesbury in 1787, he returned home and began witnessing and preaching wherever he could find an audience. In 1788 he was received into the Methodist ministry with the status of being "on trial" and assigned to the Calvert circuit in Maryland, under the guidance of Rev. Jonathan Forrest. Cook was the first native college-educated Methodist preacher in America. The next year he was teamed with Lewis Chastain and Thomas Scott to travel the Gloucester circuit in Virginia.

Cook was ordained deacon at the conference held in 1790 and assigned to serve with Daniel Hitt on the Lancaster circuit in Virginia. The year following he was paired with Lewis Chastain again, but this time they traveled the Berkley circuit in the same state.

Following the practice in Methodism in those days, a change was made again in 1792. Cook, with Seely Bunn, was sent to Pittsburgh, Pennsylvania. In this area, Methodists were under severe verbal attack led by several Presbyterian ministers in Westmoreland County, just west of Pittsburgh. Cook responded to an assault written by a man named Porter and published in a newspaper. The interchange continued for several issues.

Soon another Presbyterian, named Jamieson, challenged Cook to a public debate. This debate took place in the summer of 1792 in a wooded area where a large crowd gathered. A Methodist minister, A. Banning, was a co-moderator with a Presbyterian minister of the debate. Cook was so effective in his defense of Methodist doctrines that he won the support of the mostly Calvinist crowd, and his opponent left the scene. From then on it was much easier for Methodist preachers to find willing listeners wherever they went. Banning later published a report of this debate.[18]

Cook was ordained elder in 1793 and promoted to the position of presiding elder over Northumberland, Tioga, Wyoming, and Seneca Lake circuits in Pennsylvania. The next year he was moved east to preside over another district comprised of the Bristol, Chester, Philadelphia, Lancaster, Northumberland and Wyoming circuits. In 1795 he was given charge of fewer circuits to superintend: Northumberland, Wyoming, Tioga and Seneca. The following two years he moved to western Pennsylvania and presided over Clarksburg, Ohio, Redstone, Pittsburgh and Greenfield. While serving this district, Cook began a new method of dealing with seekers, he had them bow at a bench near the pulpit to be counseled and prayed through to victory. This procedure soon became a regular feature of Methodist revival meetings and continues to the present time.

Due to the physical breakdown of Poythress, Bishop Asbury appointed Cook as presiding elder of Methodist circuits in Kentucky. Shortly after Cook's arrival, and due to the resignation of Metcalf, Asbury appointed Cook principal of Bethel Academy.

Because a restructured Transylvania College in Lexington, Kentucky was drawing a number of students to its campus, the Methodists reacted by requesting Cook to upgrade Bethel Academy to a higher academic level. Latin, Greek, classical literature, and Bible courses were taught and the number of students increased (no record remains of the number involved). But Cook was outspoken in his opposition to slavery, whereas Metcalf and some of the trustees were not. Early in 1800 Cook was either fired or chose to cease teaching at Bethel Academy.

Before Cook left Bethel Academy, he met and married on November 9, 1799, Tabitha Slaughter, daughter of Lt. James and Elizabeth Slaughter, of nearby Mercer County.[19] In 1800, Valentine and Tabitha Cook moved to Harrodstown (Harrodsburg), county seat of Mercer County, where he began teaching in a school for boys. He dropped his itinerant relationship with the Methodist Church and located, i.e., he ceased pastoring a church but preached whenever he was asked. Soon his widowed mother and two of his brothers moved to a farm in Mercer County, but Valentine was restless and moved several times. A deed, dated April 25, 1803, gives information that Valentine and his wife paid $1,260 for two hundred acres in Washington County, which bordered Mercer County to the west.[20] Apparently his farm was close enough to the county line that he could marry fourteen couples in 1805 in Mercer County.[21]

In either 1806 or 1807 Cook and his family moved to a farm near Russellville, Logan County, Kentucky. His log house served as both a home and a school for boys. He was also active as a preacher; he and Rev. Phillip Kennerly of Virginia started a second Methodist church, called Kennerly's Chapel, in the county.

The campmeeting movement had started in Logan County in July, 1800 under the leadership of a Presbyterian minister, Rev. James Gready and two brothers; John McGee, a Methodist preacher and William McGee, a Presbyterian preacher. Campmeetings sprang up throughout central Kentucky and in neighboring states.

Cook gave his full energies to promoting this new form of evangelism. Evidently some of these activities placed a measure of obligation on the Western Conference, for there are notations in several conference minutes relating to monies paid to, and some owed Cook. The Journal of 1808 notes five dollars were paid to Cook,[22] and this statement: "Lawner Blackman proceeded to read a letter addressed to Valentine Cook on the subject of his Mission, in which he is informed that the Conference will pay him when able."[23]

The journal for 1809 has in its report of the Committee on Appropriations this note: "Paid Volentine [sic] Cook $50. It being part of $75 due him from the Conference."[24]

A controversy with some Baptist preachers in Logan County over the practice of baptism involved Cook, who was slow in bringing his converts into the Methodist Church. A Baptist, Mr. V--- enjoyed this opportunity to convince these converts that they ought to be immersed and join the Baptist Church. He ridiculed Cook's position that it was valid to baptize converts by sprinkling or pouring water on the head, and that children of Christians should be baptized. A public debate was arranged between the two men and Cook easily won. Dr. Edward Stevenson published the text of Cook's arguments but provided no place or date for the debate.[25]

Valentine and Tabitha Cook were the parents of eleven children: James, b. circa 1800, Jessamine County, Ky.; Richard H., b. circa 1802, Jessamine County; Valentine,

b. circa 1804, Washington County ? ; Gabriel S. b. circa 1806, Logan County, KY.; Nancy, b. circa 1806, Logan County; Eliza A. b. circa 1810, Logan County; Rev. Thomas F. b. 1813, Logan County; Rev. John F., b. 1814; William M. b. circa 1816; Susan Bell, b. Jan. 5, 1820, Logan County; Franklyn (Francis) Asbury, b. circa 1821-22, Logan County.[26]

Excerpts from a letter written by Rev. Thomas Scott provide insight about the Rev. Valentine Cook:[27]

Chilicothe, O., May 16, 1851

My Dear Sir; I became acquainted with Rev. Valentine Cook first in the autumn of 1789, when I suppose he must have been not far from twenty-five years of age. I knew him ever afterwards until he was summoned away to his eternal rest. He was undoubtedly, in several respects, one of the remarkable men of his day.

As to his personal appearance—standing erect, his height was about six feet; his limbs were straight, muscular and well proportioned; his breast and shoulders broad; his complexion very dark; his hair thick, black and curly; his eyes also black, and when excited, very piercing; his eyebrows and eyelashes dark and heavy; and his mouth uncommonly large. His general appearance was altogether imposing, indicative at once of great activity and strength. His movements when walking resembled those of the Indians, or former hunters of the West—the foot was drawn directly up, thrown forward, and then placed firmly upon the ground with the almost noiseless movement of a cat, and the eyes were alternatively moving from side to side, that no object embraced within the range of his vision might escape his observation.

He was slovenly in his dress, and ungraceful in his manners and conversation, but not discourteous. He seldom smiled; but when he did, it was an odd, freakish, whimsical kind of smile that I am at a loss for words to describe. He was one of the most absent-minded men with whom I have ever been acquainted....

Several of his intellectual organs were finely developed, but this was by no means true of all. He had in his constitution a dash of both enthusiasm and superstition; and it was sometimes difficult to determine, by his actions, whether he had or had not passed that very delicately drawn line, which separates eccentricity from the lower species of monomania.

Mr. Cook's Christian and ministerial character was in every respect most exemplary. He was humble, tractable, patient, and faithful in the discharge of every private, social and ministerial duty. He professed, and I doubt not enjoyed, uninterrupted communion with the Father and the Son, through the Blessed Spirit. His efforts for the salvation of his fellow-men and the extension of his Redeemer's Kingdom were seldom, if ever, surpassed. He always found ready access to the hearts of the people. Great multitudes, during his ministry, acknowledged him as their spiritual father. If you ask whether he was an eloquent man, I should say that, if the effect produced upon an audience be the true test of eloquence, he was surpassingly so. His articulation was distinct, his emphasis correct, and his thoughts well arranged and well expressed; but his very rapid and vehement mode of utterance sometimes produced an unpleasant gutteral sound, as if he were gasping for breath. But there was an unction about his manner that rendered his preaching quite irresistible. On several occasions, I witnessed large congregations completely bowed and overwhelmed by the alternate tenderness and pungency of his appeals. Arrows that pierced to the centre of the soul seemed to be flying in every direction. Some were weeping, trembling and praying; others falling prostrate and crying for mercy; others struggling into the liberty of God's children; while others were singing or shouting for joy....

Mr. Cook read, prayed and reflected much. He was familiar with the writings of Wesley, Fletcher, Watts, Stackhouse, Prideaux, Baxter, Bunyan, Young, Milton, and several of the most distinguished German authors, who flourished about the time of the Synod of Dort. He was well acquainted with the doctrines of the Gospel, as held by his own Church, and always seemed ready to engage for their defense; but, on some other subjects, I used to think that he sometimes evinced a lack of discrimination and good judgment....

In the summer of 1819 he felt a premonition he would not live much longer, so he decided to make a trip alone by horseback back East where he began his ministry and then visit his boyhood home. He left that fall and returned the spring of the next year.

He preached at many places as he traveled, including Lexington, Kentucky; Cincinnati, Ohio; Pittsburgh, Pennsylvania; New York City; Philadelphia, Pennsylvania; and Baltimore, Maryland, where he spent most of the winter. A revival broke out in the city that lasted many weeks. On his way home he stopped in Greenbrier County, West Virginia, visiting friends, and relatives and the graves of his parents.

In 1822, after preaching at a campmeeting near his home in Logan County, he returned home where he was attacked by a severe fever. Shortly before he died, he exclaimed, "When I think of Jesus and of living with Him forever, I am so filled with the love of God that I scarcely know whether I am in the body or out of the body." He then lost consciousness and soon expired.[28] He was buried on the Harold Frogge Farm, Logan County.[29]

On Sunday, July 29, 1934, The Louisville Annual Conference Historical Society, Methodist Episcopal Church, held a celebration in memory of Rev. Valentine Cook and of the beginning of Campmeetings at Muddy River, near Russellville, Logan County, Kentucky. At the morning worship service, Bishop U.V.W. Darlington preached, and at the afternoon service, Rev. Summers Brinson read a biography of Valentine Cook.[30]

The climax of the afternoon service was the unveiling of this inscription:

In Memory of Rev. Valentine Cook, A.M.
1763-1822
Pioneer Methodist Preacher
Admitted on Trial 1788
Ordained Deacon 1790, Elder 1793, Located 1800
He was a man of great learning and genuine piety.
Due west of this place 500 yards is the site of the first
Camp Meeting held in the world in July, 1800.
Erected by the Louisville
Annual Conference Historical Society
July 29, 1934

NATHANIEL HARRIS

Unfortunately, information about Rev. Nathaniel Harris is limited, though he might be termed the unsung hero of Bethel Academy. Without his faith and persistent efforts, the school would surely have ended in 1804, but his vision was not blinded, he was instrumental in raising a new Bethel Academy from the abandoned frame of the original structure.

Nathaniel Harris was born August 29, 1759, in Powattan County, Virginia, of well-to-do Presbyterian parents. In his youth he indulged in the popular sins of his day. He served his state in the Revolutionary War and was at the battle of Guilford Courthouse, North Carolina.

Nathaniel was converted in August 1783 and joined the Methodist Church. He soon felt a call to preach and served the church for many years as a local preacher. He moved to Fayette County, Kentucky, in 1790, in the section that later was to become Jessamine County. As a local preacher he was active throughout the area and on March 14, 1799, he had the honor of marrying the first couple in the newly formed Jessamine County. He continued to marry and bury many people, and preach many sermons throughout more than sixty years of ministry.

B.H. Young honors him with these words:[31]

He preached in the various towns of Central Kentucky, and in administering to the afflicted and the sick none ever excelled him. At marriages and funerals his presence was always sought, because of his tender sympathy and because of the love and confidence manifested towards him. He founded several Methodist churches in Jessamine County.... He was a faithful, earnest, devout man of God. Some might call his sphere humble, but his influence on the religious and moral condition of Jessamine County will long be felt, and in it he has a monument, which should be both to his church and to those of his name, a cause of unfailing pride.

From the beginning of the operation of Bethel Academy in 1794, he was appointed a trustee of Bethel Academy and in a few years became the president of that Board. In 1800 he and his family moved to Bethel Academy and conducted school until 1803 and possibly through the spring of 1804. He was chairman of the committee that brought charges against Rev. John Metcalf for removing furniture in late 1803 or early 1804 from the abandoned Bethel Academy and won a judgment from the Methodist Quarterly Conference at Lexington, Kentucky, that Metcalf should be suspended from ministerial duties for twelve months.

As chairman of the trustees of Bethel Academy, Harris oversaw the buying of four lots in Nicholasville, the razing of the Bethel Academy building, the moving of materials from that site to Nicholasville, and the construction of a structure for a revitalized Bethel Academy. This event happened from 1818 to probably 1821. During this time, Harris lived on a 200-acre farm on Hickman Creek which he bought for $800 in 1811.[32] Harris joined the Ohio Methodist Conference in 1820 and was appointed to the Lexington circuit.[33] In 1822 he was transferred to preach on the Frankfort-Danville circuit, then was appointed to Paris, Kentucky in 1823. The 1824 minutes lists him as having located, i.e., he ceased to serve as a pastor but could preach as he had opportunity.[34] He moved to Versailles where he lived with two unmarried daughters. His will is dated May 25, 1848, and in it Harris mentions two sons and four daughters: Nathaniel, Asbury, Jane Harris Wright, Elizabeth A. Harris Griffin, Ann and Mary. Harris died August 12, 1849, lacking a few days of being ninety. His will was probated at the September Woodford County Court, 1849.[35]

RICHARD MASTERSON

Mr. Masterson was born in Virginia of a prominent family and married Sarah Shore July 29, 1784, and brought his family to Kentucky soon afterwards. In 1786 he came under the ministry of James Haw and Benjamin Ogden, was converted and built a log structure that became the first Methodist church in Kentucky. The place was called Masterson Station near Lexington, Kentucky. The first Methodist Conference held in Kentucky was conducted by Bishop Francis Asbury in May 1790. It was at this conference, in his building that the decision was made to build Bethel Academy. Several other annual conferences were held at Masterson Station during that decade.

In 1796 Mr. Masterson sold his farm and moved to Carrol County on the Ohio River near Carrollton, but he continued to buy and sell property in Fayette County.[36] The congregation at Masterson Station scattered soon after their move and the building fell in disrepair.

His home in Carroll County was a resting place for many Methodist preachers, however, he was also the owner of many slaves. He died March 31, 1806, and his wife, Sarah, died September 12, 1834.[37]

JOHN LEWIS

Information provided by a descendent of John Lewis, Dr. F. Willard Robinson, Lake Hughes, California, is the source of some of the data in this biography. This information is found in the article, "The Lewis Family," pp. 91-117, *The History of the Robinson Family.* This volume was both authored and published by Dr. Robinson in 1993.

The ancestry of John Lewis goes back to a grandfather, also called John Lewis, who lived in Virginia on lands at Difficult Run in Loudoun County. The family was of

Scotch/Irish heritage.

The John Lewis of interest here was born in 1738, fourth son of Thomas and Elizabeth Mealy Lewis. When John married a girl named Elizabeth, between 1760 to 1762, he was given part of the family property. Here their three boys: William, Thomas, Joshua and probably daughter Ann were born.

John with his father served as Episcopal Churchwardens in the Shelburne Parish and heard Bishop Asbury preach when he visited the area between 1776 to 1781. John was converted and joined the Methodist church.

John Lewis and his father were among those who resisted the rule of the British over Virginia[38] and served on the Revolutionary Committee of Loudoun County in 1774 and 1775. Two years later, John joined the Loudoun Militia, and on May 15, 1777, was commissioned captain of the Continental Line.

John Lewis, his wife, Elizabeth, and family left their 250 acres in Loudoun county in 1783 and followed the Wilderness Trail to the Bluegrass region of the western part of Virginia. They settled on Jessamine Creek in Fayette County, in a section later to become Jessamine County. John built the first paper mill west of the Allegheny Mountains on this creek, according to the Lewis family tradition.

The extent of John Lewis' wealth is indicated by the number and size of grants of land accorded him, in recognition of his services in the Continental Army. The grants were in several of the counties in the Bluegrass area, only the instances in Fayette County are noted here:[39]

January 1, 1783, 1,000 acres surveyed on a branch of the Kentucky River.[40]

January 17, 1784, 3,000 acres on Elkhorn Creek.[41]

June 16, 1784, 8,347 1/2 acres on Elkhorn Creek but surveyed as 6,847 1/2 acres.[42]

June 5, 1786, 100 acres on Jessamine Creek.[43] This was probably the acreage he gave the Methodist Church through Bishop Asbury on May 17, 1790, for a site on which to build Bethel Academy. John Lewis also gave land for a church known as Lewis Chapel, near the Academy. This was the second Methodist church built west of the Allegheny Mountains. In 1794 the Methodist conference was held in this chapel. Other grants were the following:

June 28, 1774, 2,000 acres on Elkhorn Creek in partnership with Charles Lewis.[44]

June 30, 1774, 2,000 acres on Elkhorn Creek.[45]

June 30, 1774, 2,000 acres on Elkhorn Creek.[46]

January 28, 1783, 1,000 acres in Fayette County, Tismon Creek.[47]

March 1, 1785, 1,000 acres in Fayette County.[48]

April 11, 1785, 600 acres in Fayette County.[49]

March 26, 1784, 164 acres in Fayette County, Stoners Creek.[50]

When Bishop Asbury visited Bethel Academy for the last time in 1800, holding the annual conference there, he visited in the Lewis home. At the time John Lewis was disabled with a broken leg.[51] In the article, "The Bethel Academy Story" reference is made to deeds in which John Lewis transferred slaves to some of his children and several other people, and that he seemed to forget he had given a quit claim deed to the trustees of Bethel Academy for the 100 acres on which the school was built. He willed the 100 acres to his son William in 1816 but when he was alerted to his mistake, he gained by some means, repossession from the trustees of the Bethel Academy property and willed it again to William in 1822. At that time, the transaction was done by an attorney, for John was in Arkansas.

The Lewis' oldest son, William, was a colonel and commander of United States soldiers at the "Battle of River Raison" during the War of 1812 and later captured by the British. William was released in 1814 and settled in Lewisburg, Arkansas, where he gained the rank of general. He returned to visit his father, but died on the trip back to Arkansas. A bronze plaque was placed in his memory in Little Rock, Arkansas.

John Lewis' son Thomas was a captain of a company in the Kentucky Militia in the War of 1812 and was killed in the battle called "Dudley's Defeat" at Fort Meigs south of Detroit, Michigan, in 1813.

Lewis' son Joshua was a prominent lawyer in Jessamine County and member of the Kentucky House of Representatives in 1799, 1801 and 1803 and rose to the rank of judge. In 1805 he was appointed by President Thomas Jefferson as a Territorial Judge in charge of land claims in the recently acquired Louisiana Territory, and in 1812 became a judge of the Supreme Court of Louisiana. In 1816 he ran for Governor of Louisiana but lost by sixty-one votes. He died June 5, 1833.

The Lewis' daughter Ann, who married Thomas Henning, was the mother of one girl, and died at the age of twenty-five. The youngest daughter, Mary, married a man whose surname was Shortridge. She died in Missouri in the 1830s.

The exact date of the death of John's wife is not known, but seems to have been sometime between 1813 and 1819. Likewise, the exact date of John's death is unknown, though it was sometime between 1825 and 1827.

Notes

1. Charles Ludwig, *Francis Asbury: God's Circuit Rider*, Appendix, Photo #10.

2. E.G. Swem, *The Virginia Historical Index*, vol. 2 (Roanoke, VA: The Stone Printing and Manufacturing, Co), p. 486.

3. Thomas Scott, "The Rev. Francis Poythress." *Western Christian Advocate* (Cincinnati: April 9, 1841), p. 1.

4. W.W. Sweet, *The Rise Of Methodism in the West* (New York: The Methodist Book Concern), p. 81.

5. Ibid., p. 82.

6. Ibid., p. 87.

7. E.T.Clark, *The Journals and Letters of Francis Asbury, vols. I and II* (Nashville: Abingdon Press).

8. E.G. Swem, *The Virginia Historical Index*, pp. 203-204.

9. *Kentucky's Bicentennial Family Register*, eds. J. Winston Coleman et. al. (Frankfort: America's Historic Records, Inc.), p. 269.

10. *Minutes of the Methodist Episcopal Church*, pp. 37, 40, 41, 46, 48, 50.

11. See the text of these letters in the article, "The Bethel Academy Story," in this issue of *The Asbury Theological Journal*.

12. B.H. Young, The History of Jessamine County, Kentucky (Louisville: Courier-Journal Job Printing Co., 1898), pp. 79-85.

13. N. Bangs, A History of the Methodist Episcopal Church, vol. 2 (New York: T. Mason and G. Lane), p. 440.

14. Sweet, *The Rise of Methodism*, pp. 73-207.

15. See the article, "The Bethel Academy Story" in this issue of *The Asbury Theological Journal*.

16. H.C. Teater, *Jessamine County Kentucky Cemetery Records*, vol. 1, p. 93.

17. *Deed Book I* (Jessamine County Court House, Clerk of County Court), pp. 464-465.

18. A. Banning, "Controversy Between Rev. Valentine Cook and Mr. Jamieson in 1792," *Western Christian Advocate*, vol. III, 23(September 25, 1840): 1.

19. *Marriage Bonds 1798-1807* (Mercer County Court House, Clerk of County Court).

20. *Deed Book 5* (Mercer County Court House, Clerk of County Court), p. 68.

21. *Marriage Book* (Mercer County Court House, Clerk of County Court), p. 104.

22. Sweet, *The Rise of Methodism*, p. 145.

23. Ibid., p. 147.

24. Ibid., p. 166.

25. Edward Stevenson, *Biographical Sketch of the Rev. Valentine Cook, A.M. with an Appendix, Containing His Discourse on Baptism* (1858), pp. 105-201.

26. *Cook Genealogy*, pp. 31-36.

27. Thomas Scott, "Valentine Cook," *Annals of the American Pulpit*, ed. W. B. Sprague, vol VII (1960), pp. 154-157.

28. Stevenson, *Biographical Sketches of the Rev. Valentine Cook*, p. 154.

29. *Kentucky Cemetery Records*, vol. 1, p. 291.

30. Bulletin entitled, "In Memory of Rev. Valentine Cook, A.M. 1763-1822 and Celebration of the Rise of Camp Meetings" (Louisville Annual Conference [Methodist] Historical Society, Sunday, July 29, 1934).

31. Young, *The History of Jessamine County*, pp. 209-210.

32. *Deed Book C* (Jessamine County Court House, Clerk of County Court), p. 46.

33. Kentucky was a district of the Ohio Conference from 1811-1821.

34. *Minutes of Annual Conferences...* op. cit.

35. *Will Book N* (Woodford County Court House, Clerk of County Court), p. 385.

36. *Deed Book A* (Fayette County Court House, Clerk of County Court), pp. 344, 514, 516, 517 and *Deed Book B*, p. 492.

37. W.E. Arnold, A History of Methodism in Kentucky, vol. 1, pp. 46, 47, 178, 179.

38. E.G. Swem, *The Virginia Historical Index*, vol. 2, p. 58.

39. The list of these grants are found in *Virginia Grants*, p. 76.

40. Ibid, book 2, p. 25.

41. Ibid, book 3, p. 155.

42. Ibid, book 3, p. 371.

43. Ibid, book 4, p. 300.

44. Ibid, book 1, p. 350.

45. Ibid, book 1, p. 361.

46. Ibid, book 3, p. 3.

47. Ibid, book 7, p. 36.

48. Ibid, book 8, p. 275.

49. Ibid, book 12, p. 36.

50. Ibid, book 13, p. 93.

51. E.T. Clark, *The Journals and Letters of Francis Asbury*, vol 1, p. 253.

CHAPTER 4:
THE SPADE UNCOVERS
BETHEL ACADEMY

G. HERBERT LIVINGSTON

For one hundred and forty-five years, the foundations of Bethel Academy lay largely covered with the debris of its razing in 1820. A few stones had been removed from its partially exposed south side, and a few stones from its northeast corner had been fashioned into a monument in the mid 1930s. Otherwise, neither the dimensions nor the configuration of its foundation was accurately known, not even by Bishop Asbury who held annual conferences in it several times.

In the late fall of 1964, Dr. Howard Shipps, at that time the professor of Church History at Asbury Theological Seminary, Wilmore, Kentucky, mentioned to me his interest in Bethel Academy. We agreed to take shovels to the site so we could dig in the debris, searching for hidden foundation walls. We hoped to establish the true dimensions of the foundation.

After obtaining permission from the owners of the land on which the site is located on the Jessamine County side of the Kentucky River, we went to the site and began digging. I knew from experience gained from helping at an excavation of Ramat Rahel, Israel, in 1959 that one should start a narrow trench at the low edge of a mound of debris and work toward the higher elevation of a mound. The debris at Bethel Academy rose only a few feet above the surrounding land, so we figured it would take but a short time to dig the trench.

We started at the east end of the south side and dug the trench toward the north. Basically, we found broken brick and plaster in the debris, which could be removed quite easily and tossed aside. We had dug the eighteen-inch wide trench only four feet when we found the well laid stones of a wall thirty-two inches wide. We then went to the north side and started a trench. We had the same result; a wall thirty-two inches wide. Stretching a tape from the outer edge of the north wall to the outer edge of the south wall, we had a measurement of thirty-five feet.

We next moved to the east side and began a trench toward the west. A wall twenty-four inches wide soon came to light. The same was true of our efforts at the west end of the mound of debris. Our tape revealed a length of eighty-six feet. Why someone at an earlier time had failed to do the simple task of digging four small trenches and making an accurate measurement of the foundation is puzzling.

Discussing what to do next, Dr. Shipps and I decided I should propose an excavation project to my class, "Archaeology of Palestine," which was scheduled for the spring quarter of 1965. The lectures and readings of the class agenda could be paired with weekend sessions at Bethel Academy. Several goals seemed achievable: 1) An application of the methods of archaeology to a nearby site of historic interest; 2) Gaining factual knowledge about the history of Bethel Academy from the walls and artifacts; 3) Correlating these facts with written documents related to the school.

When the class of ten students heard of the project, they were enthused. Soon a procedure of operation was worked out, with some working at the site and some working at a simple laboratory in a room provided by the Seminary.

WHERE ARE THE REMAINS OF BETHEL ACADEMY LOCATED?

From Wilmore, Kentucky, one must take State Road 29 south almost two miles to a junction with Handys Bend Road. One must turn left onto this narrow, winding road and follow it for about a mile and a half. Here on the right is a row of mobile and permanently built homes, on the left is a cluster of farm buildings. Just past a fence extending to the right is a narrow two track road. This road follows the fence about 500 feet. At the far end of the road is a shallow, wooded drainage depression which is dry, except after heavy rains. One must pass through another farm gate and at the other side of the drainage depression, enter an open pasture for cattle. To the right of the two track road, and up a gentle slope is a cluster of trees and brush. In the midst of these trees and brush are the ruins of Bethel Academy. The ruins are located at almost exactly 900 feet above sea level. The exact position is longitude 37 degrees, 44' 22"; latitude 84 degrees, 40', 10".

Visitors to the site should always get permission from the owners of the land. This permission was always generously granted to our classes, whenever they met there for excavation of the site. In 1993 the land was sold, and though the new owner is willing to grant permission to visit the site, brush, brambles and high grass make access difficult.

WHAT QUALIFICATIONS DID I BRING TO THIS NEW PROJECT?

For a long time I had read extensively in archaeological books and journals as background to my courses in Old Testament at Asbury Theological Seminary, since I joined its faculty in 1953. Also, while serving as the first director of the Institute of Holy Land Studies in Jerusalem, Israel, in 1959, I had the privilege of working under the guidance of Dr. Johanan Aharoni at his excavation of Ramat Rahel three miles south of Jerusalem. This archaeologist later became one of the most famous Israeli experts in his field.

Learning Dr. Aharoni's methods was exciting, and helping to uncover a significant royal palace, stirred in my system the thrill of discovery by digging. At the time, the Israeli excavators focused on structures, and determined dates by a careful analysis of pottery found at a site. In that first season at Bethel Academy, I followed the same methodology.

Members of my class began digging April 10, 1965. The goals of the project were to uncover the tops of as many of the main walls as possible, and to save, clean, and identify all the cultural artifacts that came to light.

The class members were divided into two-person teams and assigned to remove weeds, vines, and brush with hand sickles and swinging scythes. The teams then removed soil from the top of the northern wall, which was labeled Wall A. At the same time, it was decided to tag the east wall as Wall B, the south wall as Wall C, and the west wall as Wall D. Hopefully, cross walls would be found and given tag letters later. Carefully plying shovels, hoes, trowels and whiskbrooms, portions of all the main walls and six interior walls were brought to light, carefully cleaned, and photographed.

We gave the letters: E, F, G, H, I, and J to the interior walls, moving from west to east. (See Figure 1 on page 80).

Each wall was built of blocks of unmortared stones, roughly dressed, the larger ones on the sides and the smaller stones on the inside of the wall. At the northeast corner, where Walls A and B joined, a number of stones had been removed. Presumably, these were used to erect the monument nearby. The portion of Wall A between Walls F and G was ascertained to be at its original height. The same was true of some of the west end of Wall C, and parts of Walls D, F, and I.

A variety of hand-made nails, thin broken glass (probably window pane), pieces of broken pottery and chinaware, whole and broken brick and broken plaster were collected in paper bags and labeled as to the place of discovery. Some class members chose to work at the sink in the laboratory, cleaning these artifacts, writing up identifying tags, and placing them according to kind in plastic bags. A recording book was used to list each artifact, giving each a serial number, starting with 01, stating where on the site it was found and a description of the artifact.

Each day I filled out a sheet, giving date, name of site, the areas assigned for excavation, the names of the diggers and a summary of what was accomplished. At the end of the working day, which was usually from eight a.m. till noon, each student made out a report about the task assigned. The site was named, what was done and what was found.

The class agreed the project was an exciting way to learn archaeology the hard way. This work brought to life what was done by experts in Palestine.

The class in the spring quarter of 1966 responded with the same enthusiasm to the excavation project at Bethel Academy. One team moved north along interior crosswall labeled G and at the half way mark the foundation of a fireplace was found. On the east side of this wall, two unmortared, stone walls extended out three feet. A mixture of ash and lime filled the space between these two walls. At the front of these two short walls and the ash/lime fill, were three parallel rows of unmortared brick six courses high. Directly opposite on the west side of Wall H was a matching fireplace, but lacking the brick facing.

A foundation of sorts was found extending out from the north face of Wall A for eleven feet, six inches, and was labeled K. It was made of two parallel rows of half-bricks, four inches high and spaced four inches apart. A cap of full bricks, eight inches long, had been laid across the parallel rows of half-bricks. Dirt filled the space between the rows, but no mortar was used in its construction. This structure touched Wall A eighteen inches west of the center of Wall A, and its top was eight inches below the top of that wall. No other structure matching this one has been found along the north side of Wall A. The function of Wall K is unclear.

A portion of mortared brick wall was found on top of the north end of Wall F. It was a double row of brick laid end to end three courses high and three feet long. Presumably, this structure was part of the wall that surmounted stone Wall F.

A turning point in my archaeological experience came in the summer of 1966. I took advantage of an opportunity to join Dr. Joseph Callaway's expedition to Et-Tell, commonly known as Ai, on the West Bank, which at that time belonged to the Kingdom of Jordan. The excavation began early in June and lasted for eight weeks. Because I already had some archaeological experience, Dr. Callaway briefed me concerning his method of digging and assigned me to supervise the excavation of Area G. I also worked with him during the summer of 1968 at the same site, supervising the excavation of areas H and K.

Dr. Callaway had worked with Dr. Kathleen Kenyon at Jericho and with Dr. G. Earnest Wright at Shechem. He then earned his doctorate at the Institute of Archaeology, University of London, in England. He was an expert in the Wheeler-Kenyon procedures of excavating a mound of debris. He taught me how to lay out a grid of squares, how to remove soil a layer at a time in one meter wide strips, how to recognize and tag each layer preserved in a balk, how to find and place in tagged containers the artifacts discovered, how to a find stone wall in a pile of stones, how to make drawings of every structure brought to light, how to sketch on graph paper the layers preserved in the balks, how to clean structures for photography, how to clean and identify artifacts, then register them properly in a record book, how to glue pottery sherds, in order to restore the original clay objects as completely as possible.

In the spring quarter of 1967, I told my class of nine students about my experiences at Et-Tell the previous summer, and how I would follow this newly learned procedure at Bethel Academy.

On paper, I had already drawn a map of the foundations of Bethel Academy and had superimposed on the map a proposed grid. To achieve my goal of having every wall overlapped by a three-foot wide balk (also known as a catwalk), I laid out six rows of three "squares" each. I squeezed some of the "squares" into rectangles thirteen by sixteen feet, whereas the true squares were sixteen feet on each side. Each square was labeled with a Roman numeral, starting with I for the square at the northeast corner and moving south along Wall B. The next row to the left, facing south, began with Square IV, and so forth.

On site, careful measurements located the lines of each balk, and at the corners of each square, forty penny nails, each of which pierced a used Coke bottle cap and a three inch square of red plastic, were hammered into the ground. These nails remained in place year after year. At the square where digging was planned, a strong cord was tied to the nails, outlining the area to be dug, and removed at the end of each day of excavation.

Because the area of a square was too large to excavate in one season, I subdivided a square into smaller units called loci. A locus (sing. form) could vary in size and a square could be subdivided into several loci, each was given an Arabic number to identify it. These loci were also outlined with nails and cords to control the area of digging. As digging progressed, the edges of the hole were repeatedly trimmed with a small pick and trowel to keep each side perpendicular to the string.

The top layer, usually only a few inches thick, was removed over the entire locus, and the soil was put through a sieve. The artifacts found in the sieve were placed in a paper bag, with a label identifying the locus and layer. The same was true of the next two layers. Occasionally, close to the walls, a fourth layer was found. The average depth to undisturbed soil ranged from twelve to twenty-four inches.

At the end of each day's work, reports were made out, drawings were made of structures, photographs were taken, and the hole backfilled enough so cattle grazing in the pasture would not be injured, should they wander through the site area.

Because some of the walls had been robbed of stones, and the level of the debris varied, there was a need for an elevation reference marker whenever drawings were made of the sides of walls, sides of structures, or the side of locus holes. This reference marker was provided by using a ten-foot length of clear plastic tubing. When needed, the tubing was nearly filled with water tinted with vegetable dye. One of the students would hold one end of the tube so that the water level in the tube matched the top edge of a wall that had not been robbed. Another student would hold his end of the tube beside a stake placed at the corner of the item to be drawn. When the water level matched the top of the unrobbed wall, the stake was marked. A stake at another part of the item to be drawn was marked at the same level and a string stretched from stake mark to stake mark. This string was called a data or elevation line and was an integral feature of all drawings made. All perpendicular and horizontal measurements were related to this string. This data line and measurements were transferred to grid paper, so that the drawing was made according to a chosen scale, usually one foot reduced to one inch. Thus all drawings had the same datum line and could easily be compared.

For several years the main goal was to dig in scattered squares, in small locus areas, to find evidence of cellars for storage of food raised in gardens near the school. No cellar was brought to light in any of the rooms of the building.

Uniformly, there were at least three strata (layers) at each locus. The first (top) stratum was black humus of two to four inches in thickness. The second stratum was the debris resulting from the razing of the building in 1820, and was made up of broken or whole bricks, mixed with broken plaster. It ranged from six to twenty-four inches in thickness. Neither stratum yielded many artifacts. The third stratum was dubbed the "gold strip," because, though only a few inches thick, it yielded a number of artifacts from the time the school was functioning. Near the walls there was the fourth stratum of loose dirt mixed with limestone chips, but no artifacts. This dirt had probably been thrown from a foundation trench.

Since the Bethel Academy building was a somewhat reduced replica of Cokesbury College, a search was made for pictures and drawings of the building in which it was housed. Pictures of this building showed a feature that was of interest to us; its roof line had four chimneys. At Bethel we had already located the foundations of two central fireplaces. Could there be two more fireplaces? The main goal for several years was to locate and bring them to light. A working assumption was that one should be close to the east end and one near the west end of the Academy building.

If this assumption were correct, the eastern fireplace should be connected to Wall J. In 1970, we determined to dig inside Wall B in Square II, and if necessary, remove the balk between II and V. In the middle section of Wall J, a double fireplace was found, one on each side of the wall. As we suspected, we had to remove a portion of the balk between Squares II and V, to bring it fully to view. Mortar still remained on top of the fireplace, providing a "footprint" of the structure above the fireplace foundation. A check at the west end of the building assured us that Wall E had at its center a matching double fireplace. Several years were devoted to excavating around these fireplaces, and a number of artifacts were found adjacent to each of them.

The years 1973 through 1980 were spent working outside Wall D and Wall C. Our goal was to find possible remains of limestone bases or post holes which would indicate where a platform and step structure had been built. We hoped to find several of them. We assumed such structures would reveal where exterior doors were located. No evidence came to light in the loci dug outside Wall D and only limited evidence along Wall C. Near the center of this wall, there was one flat stone that might have supported part of a log platform, and one four-inch diameter post hole. There were no duplicates of these items.

Along Wall D some broken window glass and some handmade square nails were found, but both appeared in abundance along the outer side of Wall C. Sherds of chinaware and earthen jars that showed up here also, suggest they may have been thrown out of doors or windows.

One puzzle remained unsolved. Where was the food cooked for the principal's family and the boys? A study of practices at the end of the eighteenth century and the beginning of the nineteenth century revealed that large dwellings normally had separate buildings for kitchens to reduce a fire hazard. The trees and brush extended east of the school building farther than on the other sides, so we surmised that area was worthy of investigation.

In the fall of 1980, our class cleared this area of brush and measured ten-foot squares separated by balks two-feet wide. Nails and stout string were used to visualize these squares on the ground. A majestic maple tree dominated the central part of this grid.

We decided to begin digging in the two central squares along the north side and succeeded in clearing them by the end of the season. The depth of the debris varied from four to eight inches.

A number of chunks of limestone came to light but none joined to form a pattern indicating a foundation, except at the south edge of one square. It appeared to be a corner, but was found nearly at the end of the last day of digging. Further exploration had to wait till the 1981 season of work.

During the fall of 1981, the students worked in squares to the south of those finished in 1980. By the end of the first day, stone foundations came to light, however, they were different than those found in the main building. There were four parallel stone walls and oriented, not north to south, but northwest to southeast. The structure has been identified as the kiln in which brick were fired and limestone reduced to lime for plaster. A description of this kiln will be found in the next section of this article.

During the fall of 1985, activity was centered in the southeast room of the main building. The goal was to determine whether this room might be the dining room for those who lived at the school. The abundance of chinaware sherds and cutlery in stratum three, the "gold strip" seemed to affirm this assumption. The artifacts possibly slipped through the spaces between the floor planks as they dried and shrank.

The last session of excavation was the fall of 1990. I had been called from retirement by the Academic Dean to teach the archaeology course again. I set as my goal a search for more substantial evidence of stone bases or foundations for a porch in front of a main entrance at the center point of Wall A. The choice of location of the excavation trenches was limited by the number of medium-sized trees just north of Wall A, but a three-foot wide trench was laid out in Square VII and a similar one in Square X. The results of the work were disappointing, for no stone bases or foundations were found among the debris. Not all of that area has been dug, so some future excavation may find evidence of a front porch along Wall A.

THE STRUCTURES OF THE AUTHENTIC BETHEL ACADEMY

There are three known structures associated with the original Bethel Academy by the cliffs of the Kentucky River. These structures were the main building, the kiln and the monument on the original site. Portions of each structure still exist. This discussion will center on the basic shapes and measurements of each structure.

The foundations of the main building are thirty-five by eighty-six feet outside measurements. Walls A and C are each thirty-two inches wide. East of the center of Wall A some of the top stones are missing. West of the center of Wall A the entire wall is intact. Just west of the center of Wall A and extending to Wall G, a notch is evident on the inside top corner; it is four inches deep and five inches wide, possibly for thick joists. Wall C, between G and H, has so many top stones missing that this feature is not present, nor is it found on the inside top corner of any of the other walls.

Walls B and D are each twenty-four inches wide. Wall B is at full height only adjacent to Wall J, whereas Wall D is at full height at the portion uncovered, which is its south half. Since the ground slopes from the northwest corner to the southeast corner, the measurement of the walls from top to bottom varies from twelve inches at the northwest end of the building to fifty-two inches at the southeast end.

Walls F, G, H, and I are fourteen inches thick, except where portions of G and H form the backs of fireplaces. Here each wall is eighteen inches thick. Walls E and J are twelve inches thick, except at the location of the double-hearth fireplaces where they become twenty-four inches thick. These foundation walls have roughly dressed blocks of limestone without mortar. Presumably, they were taken from a shallow quarry about two hundred feet west of the building.

These walls form seven interior rooms on the first floor and, presumably, the same on the two floors above, giving a possible total of twenty-one rooms. In terms of foundation configuration, the first floor rooms consist of two medium-sized rooms at each end, two hall/stairways and a large, central assembly room. The four end rooms are the same size, measuring fifteen feet, six inches east to west, and fourteen feet, four inches the other way, inside the foundation walls. The hallways containing the stairs are eight feet between foundation walls. The central assembly room is thirty by twenty-nine feet.

In our records, the northeast room is labeled AA, the southeast room is BB. The eastern hall/stairway is CC, the central assembly room is DD, the western hall/stairway is room EE. The northwest room is GG and the southwest room is FF.

The two single-hearth fireplaces in the central assembly room matched each other in size and construction. Like the walls they were built of roughly dressed blocks of limestone, except the west one on Wall G had three lines of unmortared brick six courses high. The "arms" of the fireplaces were two feet wide and extended out three feet from the wall to which each was attached. The firepit was thirty inches square and filled with limestone topped with ash. In the records, the single-hearth fireplace on the east side, on Wall H is labeled 750, and west one on Wall G is labeled 1010.

The two double-hearth fireplaces matched each other and the measurements of each half matched the single-hearth fireplaces. The double-hearth fireplace between rooms AA and BB is labeled 170 and the one between rooms GG and FF is numbered 1350.

Scattered among the brick in the debris were broken, sometimes whole, brick covered with a blue/green glaze. Most of these items were near the fireplaces. The glaze was probably produced by the prolonged heat of the fires in the fireplaces, which melted the silicon in the clay and changed it to the glaze.

Near the center of Wall D three courses of three rows of mortared brick were found in place. The bottom course was set back from the outer edge of Wall D one inch. The end of each brick on the second course was molded with a gentle "s" curve, which set the brick of the third course back another three inches. A broken brick with the same kind of molded end was found at the east end of the building. Presumably, this construction was true of the brick of the second course of all four outer walls. All whole bricks found in place and in the rubble measured, with slight variations, four inches wide, eight and one half inches long and two and one half inches thick. Examples of brick covered with some plaster were taken from the debris on the inside of all exterior walls. This plaster averaged a three-eighth inch sand coat and a three-sixteenth inch finish coat. The finish coat was covered with whitewash.

The double row of mortared brick found at the north end of Wall F serves as an example of how the interior walls were constructed at least to the top of the wooden joists. An abundance of pieces of plaster near the interior walls had impressions of wooden lathe on the back side, indicating that the interior walls were constructed of wood. The plaster averaged one half inch thick for the sand coat and one eighth inch thick for the finish coat. For the most part the finish coat was covered with whitewash.

An abundance of handwrought nails, ranging in size from two penny (one half inch) to ten penny (three inches), were found in all the debris. Innumerable pieces of one-sixteenth inch thick glass, with a greenish tint, were recovered, mostly from debris outside the building.

The discovery of the kiln was a surprise. It was oriented northwest to southeast and consists of four parallel, stone foundations. In the records, these are labeled, facing north and moving from left to right, K-A, K-B, K-C, and K-D. The unmortared, limestone blocks were roughly dressed.

The width of Wall K-A and K-D is eighteen inches, Wall K-B is twenty-four inches and Wall K-C is thirty-two inches. Each is seventeen feet long and at the southeast end two rows of unmortared brick, mostly two courses, and at one place three courses high, extended across the ends of Wall K-B, K-C, and K-D.

There is an eighteen-inch space between each wall, each with several inches of wood ash along its entire length. The northwest end of each space also had two to three inches of lime on top of the ash. This lime had been found to the north of the kiln as far as ten feet away.

Evidently all brick for the main building were fired in this kiln and a number of limestone blocks were reduced to lime by the intense heat of wood fires in the eighteen-inch wide trenches between the walls. Along the west side of Wall K-A there still are several low stacks of arranged, fired bricks.

In the process of construction, the workers would have cut down trees for timber components in the main building. These components would be joists, wall studs, plank floors, rafters and roofing, as well as lumber for doors and windows. Branches could have fueled the fires in the kiln.

Quality clay was just beneath the soil and beneath the clay are layers of limestone. Water could be obtained from a nearby spring, but where could they find good sand in the vicinity? Perhaps sand had accumulated by the Kentucky River, washed down from the sandstone cliffs in the western foothills of the Appalachian mountains. If sand was not plentiful by the river, perhaps it would have been transported downstream by boat or raft. In either case, men would have had to haul the sand up a three hundred foot incline from the river to the school.

Window glass could have been brought to the building site from the East by raft or boat via the Ohio and Kentucky Rivers.

Rev. Francis Poythress deserves praise and credit for promoting the project, organizing the work crews, and for persevering four years until the building was closed in and at least the first floor finished. Yet, in retrospect, one must say the building was poorly located and oversized. It would have been wiser to have located Bethel Academy in Lexington, Kentucky, and start operations with a much smaller building.

When the original building was razed about 1820, materials were hauled to Nicholasville, so a new building could be constructed to house a school. This building was destroyed by fire in 1857 but rebuilt soon afterward. It was then either reconstructed or modernized in 1878. The five-acre campus, school building and a dwelling were sold to the town of Nicholasville in 1893 and put in use as a public school. When these two buildings were razed is unknown, but the Nicholasville Elementary School is presently located on Bethel Academy's site.

There is a mortared, limestone monument still standing on the original Bethel Academy site by the Kentucky River. It is situated directly over Wall I, just north of its center, and was erected by the Kentucky Methodist Episcopal South Conference in 1933. The stone was taken from the northeast corner Wall A and B.

The monument is on a four-by-five foot concrete slab and is four feet high, two feet thick and three feet, two inches, wide. The bronze plaque attached to its north face was eighteen by twenty inches. As mentioned previously in the article, "The Bethel Academy Story," this plaque was stolen in 1983 and never recovered.

ARTIFACTS FROM THE DIRT

The register of the artifacts found at the original Bethel Academy site contains almost three thousand entries. In many instances, more than one item of the same kind are grouped under one entry. These artifacts may be summarized under several categories: 1) Materials used in the construction of the Academy building; 2) Tools used to construct the building; 3) Items associated with the instruction given at the school; 4) Items associated with the school's furnishings; 5) The cutlery used by the occupants; 6) The ceramics and glass used in food preparation and service; 7) Items that throw light on food eaten by the occupants; 8) Personal items belonging to the occupants.

CONSTRUCTION MATERIALS

In the previous subsection, several of the materials used in the construction of Bethel Academy have been mentioned; limestone blocks, bricks, lime and sand for mortar and plaster, lumber, window glass and nails. Details of these items need not be repeated. Below is a description of the other artifacts related to the construction of the building.

Eleven wood screws were flatheaded and slotted. Seven were size #6, i.e., one and one half inches long. Three screws were found in the holes of half a door hinge. Three screws were broken. A badly rusted door lock was found, as well as three window and door latches, one brass door knob, one drawer pull and two portions of a stone window sill. One portion had a depression, perhaps for a pin hinge belonging to a window shutter.

As one would expect, horses were used by the construction workers. The artifact related to horses is a broken horseshoe of a size that suggests the horse was small.

CONSTRUCTION TOOLS

A few items were portions of tools utilized in one way or another in construction work. One was an iron hammer head with curved claws, another was the broken, seven-and-a-half inch long blade of a hand sickle. There are also six badly rusted jack knives. An interesting item is the broken tip of an auger bit two inches long and one inch in diameter. Nearby lay a three-eighth inch thick iron rod seven inches long. At the center of the rod is evidence of attachment of another rod at a ninety degree angle. Could this rod serve as the handle of the auger? Five fairly flat black stones could have been whetstones. Each had evidence of wear and each could easily fit the palm of a worker's hand.

SCHOOL ARTIFACTS
The artifacts that were related to school activities include one rusted pair of scissors. It was among the first artifacts found at Bethel Academy and the first to be entered in the artifact register. Four fragments of flat slate provide evidence of school assignments. Four broken pieces of slate pencil go well with the remnants of slate writing surfaces. Apparently these artifacts, after they were broken, slipped through the cracks between the floor planks.

SCHOOL FURNISHINGS
One item that fits this category is a crushed brass candle snuffer. The ferrule into which a handle was inserted is two inches long and one half inch in diameter. The snuffer cap is one and three-fourths inches deep and one inch in diameter.

There are a number of artifacts which are metal fragments of utensils used in the kitchen, which may have been Room AA in the northeast corner. These fragments are too small, and often too rusted, to identify specific vessels. Some fragments are thin, which may indicate pans or other containers. Other fragments are from one-eighth to three-sixteenths inch thick, which hint they belonged to heavier pots or kettles or frying pans. In each case the fragments are too small to provide positive identification.

Other types of vessels were made of earthenware. One kind is yellowware, i.e., the baked clay is yellowish and often the glaze is yellow. Some potsherds (broken pieces) were glazed on either the outer or inner side, and some were glazed on both sides. Another kind is redware which means the baked clay is reddish. Some sherds are unglazed, but the majority are glazed on one side or the other and some on both sides with glazes which ranged from a light brown to a dark brown, from a dark gray to black. Some sherds have a salt glaze, and some have a lead glaze. On either ware, two kinds of handles were found. One is a ledge-like protrusion on the side or on the curved shoulder of the vessel. The other is a strap handle, usually from two to three inches long and one inch wide. No potsherd qualified as part of a ceramic cover for a crock or a jug.

KITCHEN CUTLERY
Artifacts witness to a variety of kitchen cutlery. Items made of iron are seriously rusted and often broken. Knife blades, averaging six to seven inches in length, are present, most with the haft, but not the handle, still intact. Spoons tend to be made of pewter but are usually broken, leaving either the bowl or the flat, smooth handle separated. One pewter spoon five inches long with a bent handle is the exception. No large forks are present, but table forks, often broken, are of iron with two tines. In

some cases, bone is still attached on one side only, the other side lost. In other instances the bone handle is intact. No fork was complete.

CERAMIC AND GLASS ARTIFACTS

The greater number of the potsherds are from table ware, which are of three types: creamware, pearlware, and porcelain. All were made in British potteries and are of the cheapest varieties. Creamware and pearlware were the products of the ingenuity of Josiah Wedgewood, who sought to mix a clay that would,when fired at a high temperature, be like porcelain. About 1762, he found that by adding ground quartz and feldspar to clay of low iron content he could produce a cream colored ware that was harder than ware previously made in England. He covered the ware with a tin (white) glaze with a yellowish tinge. It was not porcelain but people liked it.

Wedgewood kept experimenting and in 1779 found he could whiten the clay with ground flint. He also found that by adding cobalt to the tin glaze he could change its yellowish tinge to a bluish tinge. This ware became known as pearlware and soon was more popular than creamware. Sherds of each of these wares have a clear distinction between the clay body and the glaze.

British potters did not learn to make porcelain vessels until the middle of the eighteenth century. The porcelain sherds are harder and thinner and has no clear distinction between the clay body and the glaze.

The ruins of Bethel Academy have provided hundred of sherds of these tablewares, porcelain sherds being the least plentiful. None of the sherds bear potter's marks or labels. Only a small piece of one cup handle has survived, and no sherd has marks indicating spots where handles were attached to the body of cups or bowls. Many of the creamware sherds bear portions of decorative patterns painted on the vessel before the glaze was applied and the final firing done. One type is annular ware with bands or stripes of brown, yellow, dark blue, black, dark or light green encircling the vessel. Other sherds had floral patterns in light brown, yellow, green, and blue. The sherds are small, so are difficult to match, thus, preventing recovery of a full pattern. Some sherds have patterns in brown, yellow, black and light purple, which suggest geometric designs.

Sherds preserving rims and bases were also small and few could be matched. A number of such sherds have enough curvature so diameters could be determined. Rim diameters are four, five, nine and ten inches. Base diameters are one and a half, two, three, three and a half, four, and six inches. Base heights are either one-sixteenth, one-eighth, or one-fourth inches. These measurements suggest that cups, saucers, and plates are represented by the sherds. Pearlware sherds are more plentiful than creamware sherds at Bethel Academy. Most sherds were small, however, as much as six inches of rim, and in a few instances rims and bases have been joined. A distinctive rim decoration on the pearlware is called shelledge and this type in either a medium green or a dark blue is plentiful. This type of rim is always scalloped and seems to be limited to plates, soup bowls, and platters. Soup bowls are one inch deep and the sherds of platters are thicker than the others.

Rim diameters and base diameters of pearlware sherds matched those of the creamware sherds and suggest the same kinds of vessels.

Many pearlware sherds preserve indications of decoration. Annular decoration was evident by the presence of bands of red, orange, brown, yellow, blue, black, and green. These bands of color were either on or near the rim or just above the base. Almost all the bands seemed to be on the outside of the vessel.

The bits of floral design appear much like designs on the creamware with the same colors. The same is true of geometric designs. Some sherds had a medium blue design, some were large enough to show portions of the well-known "willow" pattern. Some sherds had portions of Chinese-like buildings.

The porcelain ware that preserve portions of bases indicate diameters of one-and-a-half, two, two-and-a-half, three, three-and-a-half, and four inches. The height of the bases range from one-sixteenth, one-eighth, three-sixteenths to one-fourth inches.

Many of the rim sherds are so small that it is impossible to ascertain diameters. Sherds that are large enough, an inch or more of rim length, provide diameters of three, four, five, six, and seven inches. A large proportion of the rims are slightly scalloped and wave a bit in and out, in coordination with each scallop. A smaller number of rims are straight, with no "wiggle" of the body of the vessel.

These diameters suggest cups, saucers, bowls, and small plates. Only one portion of a handle one half an inch long is among the porcelain sherds. Its cross section is oval shaped, measuring three-sixteenths by five-sixteenths inches. No body sherd or rim sherd has evidence of places where handles were attached to a vessel. The English preferred to use porcelain vessels as tea service.

All rim sherds bear decorative designs, some on the outside only, some on the inside only and some on both sides. Body sherds that have decoration follow the same placement of designs, inside and out. Some of the base sherds are large enough to show designs on the inside only. There are no potter marks or symbols on the sherds.

Colored bands, stripes, dots, dashes, pendants, and circles are usually combined in a variety of geometric designs. The designs are often painted on the outside of the vessel, whether cup or bowl, just below the rim. The colors are of various combinations of gray, brown, red, yellow, orange, or blue. Some designs show signs of fading and wear. On these sherds the paint seems to have been applied after the final glazing and firing. On other sherds the colors are bright and show no wear. Under magnification, the paint appears to have been applied before the final glazing and firing.

Other porcelain sherds, broken parts of the body of the vessel, have some geometric designs, but mostly vines, leaves and flowers. The flowers are either red or yellow, the leaves are either green or outlined with black lines. The vine pattern without flowers often encircles the vessel just below the rim on the outside and varies between yellow, light brown or red. These vines appear to be below the glaze.

Very few of the china ware sherds fit together, so a grasp of the full motif of patterns is not possible. Bits of creamware, pearlware and porcelain were recovered from all rooms in which excavation took place and around the foundations of the kiln.

Apart from the shards of window pane, there are a limited number of shards of glass vessels found at the ruins of Bethel Academy; many are small. Besides shards that appeared to come from the body of vessels, there are a few that represent the lip, neck, and sometimes a portion of the shoulder of a bottle. A few shards represent portions of the base. No complete glass vessel was recovered from the ruins.

The colors of the glass range from clear, several shades of green, a light blue to a medium brown. Reconstruction of the full shape of a vessel is not possible, but the shards available suggest bottles that could be held in one hand. No drinking vessel is clearly present in the collection of shards.

FOOD EATEN

Among the items that provide information about food the inhabitants of Bethel Academy ate are mussel shells. These mussels may have been found in or along the Kentucky River. Chicken bones and bits of eggshell are present. An interesting find is an almost intact eggshell found beneath a layer of broken brick and plaster. One piece of brick had touched the egg enough to make a hole about three-eighths inch in diameter. The shell was empty, so it was carefully transported to the laboratory and filled with wax. It has been the most popular artifact to visitors, especially children. Beside the egg were crushed egg shells and the chicken bones.

Other bones came from cattle and wild animals. Some of the latter were possibly trapped or shot and eaten. No fish bones have been identified as yet. No artifact throws light on the kinds of vegetables eaten by the occupants of Bethel Academy.

PERSONAL ITEMS

A limited number of personal artifacts in the collection can be identified. One artifact seems to be the badly rusted remains of a watch, but that evaluation is not certain. The heavy base of a pressing iron, three finger thimbles, several small pins, a copper tackhead, two marbles, a portion of a probable toy, a portion of a doll and three buckles are among the treasures.

A number of damaged buttons are in the hoard. Most are made of pewter, many with the loop on the back missing. One pewter button appears to have been misshaped when cast. The mold evidently became loose and slightly moved apart, leaving an unusable button. Seven buttons were made from bone with one hole in the center. Two others were fashioned from wood. A few buttons are brass and one is a composite of iron, silver, and glass with a loop missing on the rusty back; the silver is crimped around the circumference. The center of this button is clear glass one-fourth inch thick and has a six-pointed star, with a group of dots at its center, impressed on the back of the glass. The glass is chipped on one edge.

No coins or jewelry have been found.

In general, the artifacts unearthed at Bethel Academy correlate well with what is known of the life style and financial level of the people who migrated into Kentucky in the latter half of the eighteenth century. For the most part, the materials for construction were locally abundant and were processed with skill, within the limits of tools available. Only a few of those tools are represented in the artifact collection, and they are mostly broken. The hammerhead is complete and possibly was lost on the job.

The pieces of slate and slate pencils are typical of school equipment in frontier days, and witness to the elementary level of instruction offered at Bethel Academy. The candle snuffer and the fireplace foundations represent the limits of lighting and heating capabilities of that time. The scraps of sheet metal and cast metal provide limited clues to kinds of kitchen equipment for preparing food, as do the odds and ends of cutlery and earthen ware.

The tableware was imported from England and is of the cheapest varieties, except for the porcelain, which may represent a higher financial level for the leaders, who for the most part came from well-to-do families in Virginia. These leaders would be Francis Poythress, John Metcalf and his wife, the wife of Valentine Cook and the Nathaniel Harris family, all of whom lived at Bethel Academy for short periods of time. Still, none of the artifacts, even personal items, were of high enough quality to indicate their owners were wealthy.

An interesting feature of the excavation of Bethel Academy is that there was little need to search for a place where throwaway articles were discarded. The artifacts were found under the floors of all rooms in which digging was done. They were found all around the building, and round about the kiln.

Life was primitive on the Kentucky frontier and people were not very careful in disposing of their junk.

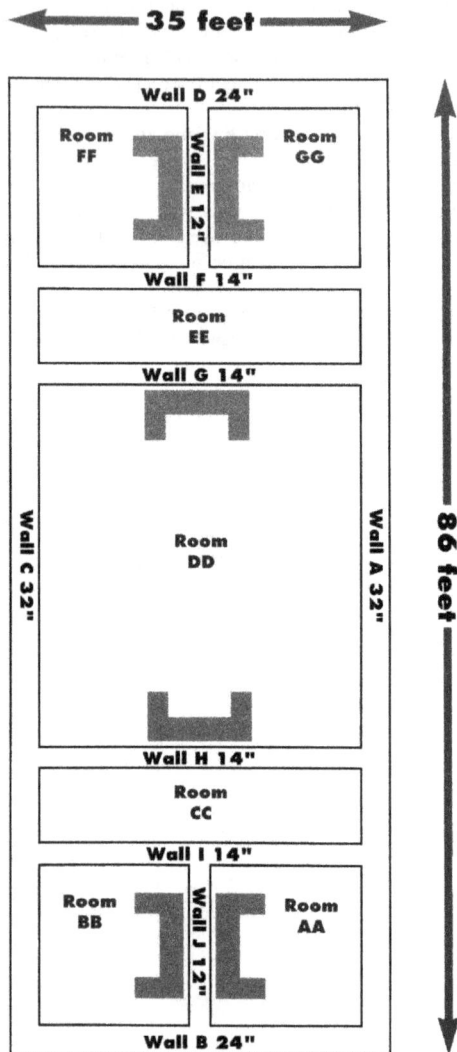

Bethel Academy
figure 1

Appendix A

Original Deed
November 28, 1797

This indenture made the twenty-eighth day of November in the year of our Lord, one thousand seven hundred and ninety-seven; between John Lewis of the County of Fayette and the Commonwealth of Kentucky and Elizabeth his wife of the one part, and the Reverend Francis Poythress now president of Bethel School in the county and state aforesaid, and his successors presidents of the said school in trust to and for the use and the profit of the said school of the other part. Whereas the said John Lewis on the sixteenth day of May in the year of our Lord, one thousand seven hundred and ninety-four did contract to and with James Hord, Nathaniel Harris and Andrew Hynes, then trustees for the said intended school called Bethel to convey to them the said Trustees and their successors one hundred acres of land situate in the county aforesaid, being part of two surveys and bounded as follows: Beginning at two cedars in James Curd's land on the cliffs of the river, running thence south sixty-one poles to a hickory and elm, thence, north thirty-seven poles to the hempmill branch, thence up the said branch its several courses to three elms thence west to James Curd's corner, and with his line same course in all two hundred and sixty poles to the beginning. Now this indenture witnesseth that the said John Lewis for and in consideration of the sum of five shillings current money to him in hand paid by the said Francis Poythress at and before the sealing and delivery of these presents, the receipt whereof he doth hereby acknowledge and for the purpose of buying the said contract into effect, hath granted bargained and sold and by those presents doth grant bargain and sell unto the said Francis Poythress and his successors in trust for the use, intent and purpose herein mentioned, all the before mentioned and described tract or parcel of land and premises containing one hundred acres with the appurtainances with every right privilege and immunity thereunto belonging or in any wise appertaining and the revision and reversions, remainder and remainders, rent issues and profits thereof, and also all the estate interest and property thereof. To have and to hold the before mentioned and described one hundred acres of land and premises with its appurtenances unto the said Francis Poythress and his successors in trust to and for the use intent and purpose herein is possessed forever to the only proper use benefit and behoof of the said Francis Poythress and his successors in trust as aforesaid forever, being president of the said school called Bethel or by whatever name or title the same shall be called or known and to and for the use benefit and behoof of the said school forever. And the said John Lewis and Elizabeth his wife for themselves their heirs executors and administrators do further covenant grant and agree to and wit the said Francis Poythress and his successors presidents of the said school called Bethel for the time being, that the said Francis Poythress and his successors in trust as aforesaid and for the use aforesaid shall have, hold, and possess the before mentioned one hundred acres of land and premises with the appurtenances and all houses and buildings erected or to be erected thereon without the let hindrance or molestation of them the said John Lewis and Elizabeth his wife or of any other person or persons whatsoever. And it is further covenanted and agreed by and between the said John Lewis and his heirs, and the said Francis Poythress in behalf of himself and his successors in trust as aforesaid that the said Francis Poythress president of the school called Bethel do and shall permit such ministers and preachers as are under the direction, and in communion with the general conference held in Baltimore or any other place and such minister or preachers are appointed at the yearly conference in Kentucky or any other part of the Western district, preach and expound God's holy word therein, and administer the ordinances of the Gospel at any time and at all times. That the said Francis Poythress and his successors do and shall permit such teacher as shall have a recommendation from the Bishop and Conference held in Baltimore or elsewhere to teach the English or other languages or sciences.

That the said Francis Poythress and successors aforesaid do appoint the Trustees for visiting and conducting the said school from year to year, to revoke and change such trustees from time to time as he or they may think proper. And it is further covenanted and agreed between the parties aforesaid that if the said Francis Poythress and his successors shall judge by the counsel and examination of and with the Trustees, that any preacher or teacher in Bethel School are either unfit for want of proper abilities or want of diligence or any impiety; he shall dismiss such persons from the employ of the said school. And it is further covenanted and agreed between the parties aforesaid that in the passage of the said Francis Poythress, or on his ceasing to be a member of the Methodist Episcopal Church, the Bishop and conference held in Baltimore or elsewhere shall appoint another person to act as president of Bethel School, who shall possess all the right and title, law and equity, and possess all the privileges and powers covenanted and granted to the said Francis Poythress by this deed. And the said John Lewis for himself his heirs executors and administrators doth further covenant grant and agree to and with the said Francis Poythress and his successors that he the said John Lewis and his heirs do, and shall well and truly make or cause to be made all such further, and other act and acts, deed or deeds, assurances and covenants in the law for the more perfect granting and assuring the promises aforesaid as shall be reasonably required by the said Francis Poythress and his successors so that the said lands and premises shall enure and be held for the benefit use and purpose of the said school call Bethel forever, according to the true intent and meaning of these presents. And lastly the said John Lewis for himself his heirs executors and administrators doth further covenant grant and agree to and with the said Francis Poythress and his successors as aforesaid, that he the said John Lewis the before mentioned lands and premises with its appurtenances to the said Francis Poythress and his successors for use of the said school shall and will warrant and forever defend by these presents. In witness whereof the said John Lewis and Elizabeth his wife for themselves and the said Francis Poythress on behalf of himself and his successors have hereunto set their hands and affixed their seals the day and year first above written sealed and delivered in the presence of

John Lewis (seal)

Elizabeth (seal)

Francis Poythress (seal)

John Metcalf

Presigned sealed and delivered this twenty-fourth day of May on thousand eight hundred and four in the presence of :

James Hord

John Lewis (seal)

James Crutcher

Thomas Wilkerson, Fayette County School

Nath Harris, Clerk's office, January 14th, 1805

This indenture of bargain and sale from John Lewis to Francis Poythress, President of Bethel School and his successor presidents of the said school proved by the oath of Nath'l Harris one of the witnesses thereto, and is certified. On the 28th day of January 1805 was proved by the oath of Thomas Wilkerson a second witness thereto and is certified. And on the 15th day of April 1805 was fully proved by the oath of James Hord a third subscribing witness thereto and is admitted to record in my office agreeably to law.

Teste, Levi Todd, Clerk

APPENDIX A-2

June 1, 1816

This indenture made this first day of June 1816 between John Lewis of the County of Jessamine and State of Kentucky of the one part and William Lewis of the state and county aforesaid of the other part witnesseth that the said John of and in consideration of the love and affection he has towards the said William, his son, and for divers other good offices done and performed by the said William to the said John hath granted bargained and given for and in consideration of a certain tract or parcel of ground situate lying and being in the County of Jessamine, commonly called and know the Bethel tract containing one hundred acres be the same more or less bounded as follows (to wit) beginning at a stake in Patrick Noonen's line on the east side of the hempmill branch running thence west to the Bethel Academy corner, thence said West Course with Bethel line passing James Curd's corner on the line and with said line same course continued two hundred and sixty-four poles in all to two cedars on the cliffs of the Kentucky River thence south sixty-one and three-fourth poles to a cedar in the edge of the cliffs thence east 266 poles to a white oak and sugar tree thence north to the beginning to have and to hold the said tract or parcel of ground together with all and singular the appurtenances thereunto belonging or in anywise appertaining to him the said William and his heirs forever free from the claim or claims of the said John

or any person claiming under him in witness whereof the said John hath set his hand and seal the day and year above.
Written teste

Richard Hightower
John Lewis (seal)
Daniel Lewis
John Lewis (seal)
Jessamine county Set.
June 1, 1816

APPENDIX A-3

May 24, 1819

Know all men by these presents that I, John Lewis, of the County of Jessamine, State of Kentucky have for and in consideration of the natural love and affection which I have and bear towards my beloved son, William Lewis, of said county and state this day given granted aliened and confirmed and by these presents do give grant alien and confirm unto my said son William his heirs and assigns forever all and every part of my distributable share or portion of the Estate real or personal of my deceased brother Daniel Lewis of the County of Fairfax, Virginia, who died without an heir to have and to hold the said share or portion of said Estate whether consisting of lands or negroes or both and every other species of Estate to the said William Lewis my son and his heirs forever and the Title to the same against the claim of any person whatsoever. I shall and will warrant and forever defend. In testimony whereof I have here unto set my hand and seal this 24th day of May, 1819.
Witness:

Daniel B. Price
John Lewis (seal)
Jessamine County
24th April 1819

The within deed of gift from John Lewis to William Lewis was this day produced before me in my office and acknowledged by the said John Lewis to be his act and deed and the same is duly entered of record.
Teste   D.B. Price, clerk
Side note: Examined and delivered, September 11th, 1820.
J.M.H.
D.Cl..

APPENDIX A-4

Second Important Deed
June 12, 1819

This indenture made and entered into this 12th day of June in the year of our Lord one thousand eight hundred and nineteen between John Metcalf and Nancy his wife of the county of Jessamine and state of Kentucky of the one part and Nathaniel Harris, Samuel H. Woodson, William Caldwell, Jesse Head, Thomas B. Scott, John Lewis, James Fletcher and Frances P. Hord, Trustees of the Bethel Academy of the other part witnesseth that the said John Metcalf and Nancy his wife for and in consideration of the sum of Three Hundred Dollars the receipt whereof they do hereby acknowledge and forever discharge and acquit the aforesaid Trustees and their successors have granted bargained sold aliened and confirmed and do by these presents grant bargain sell alien and confirm unto the said Trustees and their successors forever a certain tract or parcel of land situate lying and being in the aforesaid county of Jessamine containing two acres and bounded as follows (to wit) beginning at a stake in said Metcalf's most northwardly line and near where the most westwardly line of the late addition to the town of Nicholasville crosses the same running thence Metcalf's said line S. 89 degrees W., 20 poles to a stake in said line thence S. 1 degree E. 16 poles to a stake thence N. 89 degrees E. 20 poles to a stake in said line thence N. 1 degree w. 16 poles to the beginning and provided said Trustees or their successors cannot effect a purchase of the ground lying in front of the said two acres said Metcalf and Nancy his wife oblige themselves to open a way for said Trustees or their successor into the Town of Nicholasville whenever it shall be necessary to have and to hold the said tract of land with all its appurtenances to the only proper use and behoof of the said Trustees and their successors forever and the said John Metcalf and Nancy his wife their heirs executors and administrators do covenant and agree with the aforesaid trustees and their successors that they the said John Metcalf and Nancy his wife shall and will forever warrant and defend the right and title of said tract of land with all its appurtenances against them the said John Metcalf and Nancy his wife their heirs executors administrators and against the claim or claims of all manner of person or persons whatsoever in Testimony whereof the said John Metcalf and Nancy his wife have hereunto set their hands and seals the day and year above written.

John Metcalf (seal)
Nancy Metcalf (seal)
Jessamine county set.

The foregoing deed was on this 15th day of June 1819 acknowledged before me by John Metcalf and Nancy his wife to be their act and deed and she the said Nancy being by me examined separate and apart from her said husband freely and voluntarily relinquished her right of dower to the land and premises thereby conveyed and is thence upon duly recorded.

Teste Dan'l B. Price clk.

APPENDIX A-5

Third Important Deed
February 24, 1820

This indenture made this 24th February 1820 between Leslie Combs and Margaret his wife of the Town of Lexington of the County of Fayette and Commonwealth of Kentucky of the one part and Nathaniel Harris prest William Caldwell William Shrieve Francis P.

Hord Robert Crockett George J. Brown Archibald Young and James Fletcher of the County of Jessamine and Commonwealth aforesaid of the other part witnesseth that the said Leslie Combs and Margaret his wife for and in consideration of the sum of two hundred dollars current money of Kentucky to them in hand paid the receipt whereof is hereby acknowledged hath granted bargained and sold and by these presents do grant bargain sell and confirm unto the said Trustees and their successors in office and assigns all that tract or parcel of land situate and being in the County of Jessamine on the waters of Jessamine Creek containing about two acres more or less bounded as follows to wit lying and binding on the north side of the two acres tract or lot of land bought by said Trustees of John Metcalf in the Suburbs of the Town of Nicholasville the distance of twenty poles being the whole length of said North side thence from both corners thereof north being the same corners of the lines of said two acres tract bought of Metcalf until it intersects the south side of the cross street of the Town of Nicholasville commonly called South street running past Francis P. Hord's present residence and G.P. Welch as it is extended by said Combs and including all the land surrounded by said streets and the lines before mentioned together with all and singular the premises thereunto belonging or in any wise appertaining to have and to hold the land hereby conveyed with the appurtenances unto the said trustees and their successors and assigns forever and the said Leslie Combs and Margaret his wife for themselves their heirs executors and administrators the aforesaid tract of land and premises unto the said trustees and their successors in office and their assigns against the claim or claims of all and every person or persons whatsoever claiming by through or under Robert Johnson the original paterntee do and will forever define by these presents in witness whereof the said Leslie Combs and Margaret his wife have hereunto set their hands and seals the day and date first above written and are to pay back the original purchases money without interest in case it is taken by any better claim whatever and said Trustees which assigned are bound to defend the same.

Leslie Combs (seal)

Margaret Combs (seal)

State of Kentucky

Fayette County to wit February 25th, 1820

This indenture was this day produced to me the clerk of the court for the county aforesaid and acknowledged by Leslie Combs and Margaret his wife parties thereto be their act and deed she the said Margaret being by me privately examine separately and apart from her said husband and the law directs freely and voluntarily relinquished her right of dower in and to the premises conveyed by this indenture which is hereby certified to the clerk of Jessamine County Court.

Atte. J.C. Eodes, clk.

Jessamine County set. February 29th, 1820

The within deed from Leslie Combs and Margaret his wife to the Trustees of the Bethel Academy was this day produced to me in my office and by virtue of the certificate thereon endorsed is duly entered of record.

Teste Daniel B. Price

APPENDIX A-6

March 26, 1822

This indenture made and entered unto this day of March 1822 between William Lewis of the County of Jessamine and State of Kentucky of the one part and John Jackman, attorney-in-fact for John Lewis now of the territory of Arkansas of the other part witnesseth that for and in consideration of the sum of one thousand dollars to the said John in hand paid the receipt whereof he doth hereby acknowledged hath granted bargained and sold and by these presents doth grant bargain in sell alien to confirm unto the said William Lewis his heirs or assigns a certain tract or parcel of land situate lying and being in the county of Jessamine on the Kentucky River and known by the name of the Academy land and bounded as followeth to wit.

Beginning at a stake in Patrick Noonen's line on the east side of the hempmill branch running thence west to the Bethel Academy corner thence said west course with Bethel line passing James Curd's corner on said line and wit said line same course continued two hundred and sixty-four poles in all to two cedars on the cliff of the Kentucky River thence south sixty and three-fourth poles to a cedar in the edge of the cliffs thence east 266 poles to a white oak and sugar tree thence north to the beginning containing one hundred acres—to have and to hold the above bargained premises to the said William Lewis his heirs or assigns. And the said John doth by these presents warrant and defend the same from the claim or claims—all persons whatsoever. In testimony whereof I have this 26th day of March 1822 set my hand and seal.
Jessamine county set March 28th, 1922
                    John L. Lewis by John Jackman his attorney-in-fact
The within deed from John L. Lewis by John Jackman his attorney-in-fact to William Lewis was this day produced to me in my office acknowledged by the said Jackman attorney-in-fact for the said John L. Lewis to be his act and deed and the same is duly record. Book G p. 207
                    Atteste D.B. Price

APPENDIX A-7

April 19, 1822

This indenture of bargain and sale made and entered into this day of April eighteen hundred and twenty-two between David T. Walker of the county of Jessamine and State of Kentucky as attorney-in-fact for William Lewis of the one part and George Walker of the county and state aforesaid of the other part witnesseth that for and in consideration of the sum of three hundred and 31 on exon—Walkers, exos—Lewis; g. c. dollars the amount of the sum to me in hand paid the receipt whereof is hereby acknowledged hath granted bargained and sold and these presents doth grant bargain and sell unto the said George Walker a certain tract of land on the Kentucky River containing one hundred acres and bounded as followeth to wit. Beginning at a stake in Patrick Noonen's line on the east side of the hempmill branch running thence west to the Bethel Academy corner thence said west corner and with Bethel line passing James Curd's corner on said line. Same corner continued two hundred and sixty-five poles in all to two on the cliff of the Kentucky River thence south sixty-one and three-fourth poles to a cedar in the edge of the cliff east 266 poles to a white oak and sugar tree thence north to the beginning to have and to hold the said tract of land together with all the singular the appurtenances thereunto belonging or in any wise appertaining to him the said and his heirs forever free from the claim or claims of all and every person whatsoever in testimony whereof the said Walker as attorney-in-fact for the said Williams/Lewis hath hereunto set his hand and seal this day and year above written

Will Lewis (seal)

by David T. Walker, his attorney-in-fact

Jessamine County Set, April 19th, 1822

The within deed from David T. Walker as attorney-in-fact for Will Lewis to George Walker was this day produced before me and acknowledged by said David T. as attorney as aforesaid to be his act and deed and the same is there upon recorded.

Teste

David B. Price, clerk

Book G pp. 225-226

APPENDIX A-8

May 28, 1877

This article shows that the Trustees of Bethel Academy have agreed with A.N. Gordon as follows: The trustees lease and rent to said Gordon their school building residence and appurtenances together with the grounds on which the same are situated for the term of ten years from and after the first day of July 1877. In consideration of the premises said Gordon agrees and binds himself during said term to teach in the Academy building a male-high-school to be conducted by him and such assistants as he may deem proper to employ—the prices and terms of tuition to be determined by himself as well as the length of the sessions and all other questions pertaining to the management of the school. Also as a further consideration said Gordon is to expend fifty dollars per year during said term in repairs and improvements on the property and account for the same by proper vouchers in settlements with the trustees to be annually made. Also he is to teach during his school sessions five indigent sprightly boys to be designated by the trustees. The trustees on their part are also to expend fifty dollars per annum in repairs upon the property should such expenditures in their opinion be necessary. Should said Gordon at any time cease to reside on the property, he is then to give possession of the residence to the trustees.

The trustees agree also on their part to put the whole property including fencing and building in a state of good repair and to keep them so and to supply such school furniture as shall be proper and necessary. Said Gordon on his part is to charge and collect at the rate of one dollar per year for each pupil taught, except the five boys mentioned, in the school to be used as a contingent fund and to account to the trustees for the same. He is also to take good care of said property and to permit no depreda tivus, or trespasses on the same so far as he may be able to prevent it.

Witness the trustees of Bethel Academy by George Brown, President and A. N. Gordon, May 28, 1877, Filed May 28, 1878.

APPENDIX A-9

September 24, 1878

This deed between S.H. Noland and his wife Carrie K. Noland of the County of Jessamine and State of Kentucky parties of the first part and the Trustees of Bethel Academy of said county and State party of the second part. Witnesseth that the said parties of the first part in consideration of the opening of a twenty-foot street between said Bethel Academy lands, and the lands of A.Z. McAfee and the further consideration of one dollar cash in hand paid do hereby sell, grant, and convey to the party of the second part their successors and assigns the following described real estate to wit: a certain tract or parcel of land lying and being in the County of Jessamine and State of Kentucky and in the town of Nicholasville, Kentucky. Bounded as follows, on the north by the lot of Bethel Academy, on the east by D.W. Axline, on the south by Broadway Street and west by said New Street. Being that portion of lands of said S.H. Noland, cut off by the said Broadway Street, to have and to hold the same, with all the rights, privileges, and appurtenances thereunto belonging, or in any wise appertaining unto the second party their successors, and assigns forever with covenant of General Warranty.

Witness our hands this 24 Day of September 1878,

S.H. Noland
C.K. Noland
State of Kentucky
County of Jessamine, sct.

R.S. Perry, clerk of the county court of the county aforesaid, do certify that the foregoing instrument of writing from S.H. Noland and wife to Trustees of Bethel Academy was on the 5th day of October 1878 produced to me in my office and was acknowledge by S.H. Noland and wife Carrie K. Noland to be their act and deed and was this day lodged for record by the Grantee, which together with this certificate is duly recorded in my said office.

Given under my hand this 23rd day of Dec. 1878,

R.S. Perry c.j.c.c.
by Will T. Peyton

APPENDIX A-10

January 27, 1880

This deed between the Trustees of the Jessamine Female Institute party of the first part and the Trustees of Bethel Academy party of the second part all of Jessamine County State of Kentucky. Witnesseth that the party of the first part by its President T.B. Crutcher who, by order made and entered of second by first party is authorized to make this deed for and in consideration of twenty-five dollars cash in hand paid the receipt whereof is hereby acknowledged doth hereby bargain, sell, grant, and convey unto the second party their successors and assigns the following described real property to wit: A certain parcel of land within the corporate limits of the town of Nicholasville, Jessamine County, Kentucky bounded on the north by the Nicholasville and Jessamine County Turnpike Road on the east by a new street extending from said turnpike road to Williamson Street on the south by an old abandoned road recently discontinued by the Jessamine County Court which runs from the macademized terminus of Williamson Street in a westerly direction to a street recently opened and known as Academy Street, and on the west by said Academy Street. To have and to hold the same together with all the rights, privileges and appurtenances thereunto belonging or in anywise appertaining unto the party of the second part their successors and assigns forever with covenant of General Warranty, in testimony whereof the party of the first part by its President aforesaid T.B. Crutcher hereunto subscribes its corporate name and affixes its corporate seal. This January 27th, 1880.

Trustees of the Jessamine Female Institute

By Thos. B. Crutcher

President

State of Kentucky

Jessamine county sct.

I, R.S. Perry, clerk of the Jessamine County Court certify that the foregoing instrument of writing from the Trustees of the Jessamine Female Institute to the Trustees of Bethel Academy was on the 27th day of January 1880 produced to me in my office and acknowledged before me by Thos. B. Crutcher, President of the Board of Trustees of the Jessamine Female Institute to be his act and deed, and the same was this day ordered to record by the grantees which together with this certificate is duly recorded in my said office.

Given under my hand this 28th day of January 1880.

R.S. Perry, c.J.c.c.

by W.D. Lowry, D.C.

APPENDIX A-11

Minutes of the Board of Councilmen, Nicholasville, Ky.
July 25, 1893, pp. 257-259

A proposition was received from the trustees of Bethel Academy, which is as follows:

Whereas the system of common schools as provided by the laws of Kentucky prevails to a large extent in this section of the country and has become popular with our people and is being improved and made more efficient from year to year, and, whereas for the last five years as trustees of Bethel Academy, we have been unable to have a school taught in the building of said Academy, except to lease the same to the Board of Councilmen of the town of Nicholasville, for the purpose of having a school taught therein under the common school law of Kentucky, and whereas in our opinion it has become impossible to sustain a school at said Academy by the payment of tuition fees to the teacher or teachers thereof, and whereas as trustees of Bethel Academy, we possess a valuable real estate in the town of

Nicholasville, and money in the amount of about two thousand dollars ($2,000), which real estate and personal property is and always has been held to aid and further the cause of education, and whereas the Jessamine Female Institute located in the town of Nicholasville is and has been a source of pride and great benefit to our people, and have a debt on it which may result disastrously to that institution and our community, unless relieved of said debt, and whereas the Board of Councilmen of the town of Nicholasville is owner of a lot of land situated on Noland Street in said town at which a common school was formerly taught, but in which there is no sufficient building in which such a school can now be conducted.

Now in furtherance of the cause of education in Nicholasville and Jessamine County, the trustees of Bethel Academy propose to sell all its real estate in Nicholasville, including therewith all furniture and personal property thereon to the Board of Councilmen of the town of Nicholasville, for the purpose of a free school, being taught upon the same, for the sum of seven thousand dollars ($7,000)—fifteen hundred dollars ($1,500) thereof to be paid by the conveyance of the lot above mentioned in which a common school was formerly taught to the trustees of Bethel Academy, or as they may direct and the balance of $5,500 to be paid in three equal annual installments with interest from date at the rate of six percent per annum until paid. The interest is to be paid semi-annually to the said Board of Councilmen to execute its notes for said payments at the time said trustees of Bethel Academy executes its deed for the property sold by it to said town and said Board of Councilmen is to make a deed of the lot owned by it and exchanged as above stated when and as it may be directed by the trustees of the Bethel Academy. This proposition is made with the understanding that the Board of Councilmen of the town of Nicholasville will forever cause one or more rooms in said Academy building set apart for the education of pupils in branches of literature arts and sciences higher than is recognized as being the course of study in common schools and will provide a teacher or teachers in such rooms capable of teaching and instruction pupils in said higher branches and preparing them for college and this proposition is made with the further understanding that all the consideration received by the trustees of Bethel Academy, arising from the sale and transfer of its property as aforesaid and all its money, assets now in hand, are to be immediately invested in stock in the Jessamine Female Institute at its par value and the stock to be issued to the trustees of Bethel Academy and held by them. This proposition is made on the condition that it meet the approbation and consent of the trustees of Jessamine Female Institute and that they will agree to carry out the same so far as they are concerned.

Resolved that J.G. Bronaugh and T.B. Crutcher be, and they are hereby appointed a committee on behalf of this Board and directed to meet the Board of Councilmen of the town of Nicholasville, and make them a proposition set out in the foregoing preamble, and the board of trustees of the Jessamine Female Institute, and report their acts and the acts of said boards to this body at its next meeting.

It was moved and carried that the board of councilmen accept the above proposition as made by the trustees of Bethel Academy and that the yeas and nays be called. Whereupon the votes of E.R. Sparks, B.M. Arnett, J.D. Hughes, E.J. Young, A.K. Adcock, and W.T. Dickerson, all unanimous, voted yeas.

The trustees of Jessamine Female Institute having accepted the above proposition from the trustees of Bethel Academy, it was moved and carried that the mayor J.H. Bronaugh is empowered to carry out the proposition as made to the board and accepted by them.

APPENDIX A-12

Deed To Board of Councilmen of Nicholasville, Ky.
Deed Book #10 pp. 544, 545

This Deed between the trustees of Bethel Academy of the County of Jessamine and State of Kentucky of the first part and the Board of Councilmen of the Town of Nicholasville of the County and State aforesaid of the second part, witnesseth, that the said party of the first part, in consideration of the sum of seven thousand dollars—fifteen hundred of which is paid by the sale of a lot of land in Nicholasville on Noland Street on which a common school was formerly taught and which is to be conveyed as the first party may direct and the sum of $5,500, secured to be paid in three equal annual installments by the promissory notes executed by the second party, payable to the first party, each for the sum of eighteen hundred and thirty three 33/100 dollars, bearing interest from date of the note of six per cent per annum until paid—the interest payable Semi-annually which notes are unpaid and a lien is hereby retained on the property herein described to secure the payment thereof, do hereby sell, grant and convey to the party of the second part, its successors and assigns, the following described real estate, to wit: All that lot or parcel of land lying and being situated in Nicholasville, Jessamine County Kentucky, bounded on the North by Main Cross Street, on the East by the lots of Mrs. Minnie Patton, Geo. R. Pryor, David Moffat, District School lot White #1 in Jessamine County and short street (unnamed) running from the residence of Geo. R. Pryor to Main Cross Street, on the South by Broadway Street and on the West by Academy Street, on which is situated a dwelling and the Bethel Academy Building and also all the furniture and personal property on said lot or within the buildings thereon and owned by the party of the first part. This deed is made to the second party for the purpose of public schools in the town of Nicholasville and so reserved and it is made with the understanding and agreement on the part of the party of the second part that it will forever cause one or more rooms in the school building on said lot to be set apart for the education of pupils in branches of literature, arts and sciences, higher than is now recognized as being the course of study in Common Schools and will cause a teacher or teachers to be employed in said room or rooms, capable of teaching said higher branches and preparing them for college.

To have and to hold the same with all the rights, privileges and appurtenances thereunto belonging or in any wise appertaining, unto the second party, its successors and assigns forever, with covenant of General Warranty.

WITNESS, our hands and seal the 29 day of July, 1893

Trustees of Bethel Academy
By B. M. Arnett, President
STATE OF KENTUCKY,
COUNTY OF JESSAMINE.

I, R. S. PERRY, Clerk of County Court of the County aforesaid, do certify that the foregoing instrument of writing from The Trustees of Bethel Academy to the Board of Councilmen of the Town of Nicholasville was, on the 29th day of July, 1893, produced to me in my office, and was acknowledged by B.M. Arnett, President, to be the Act and deed of the Trustees of Bethel Academy, party thereto, and was this day lodged for record by the grantee, which, together with this certificate, is duly recorded in my said office.

Given under my hand, this 5th day of August, 1893

R.S. Perry C.J.C.C.

Notation on side of page 544:

The three notes mentioned herein have been paid and satisfied in full, and the lien retained in this deed is hereby released. This August 26th 1896

Trustees of Bethel Academy by B.M. Arnett, Pres.

Attest: Curd Lowry cjcc

APPENDIX A-13

Minutes of Board of Councilmen of Nicholasville, Ky.
August 4, 1893, p. 265

The mayor presented a deed from the trustees of Bethel Academy to the Board of Councilmen of the town of Nicholasville, which on motion was accepted by the board and ordered recorded in the proper office.

On motion the mayor appointed E.R. Sparks and A.K. Adcock a committee on repairs on Bethel Academy.

The mayor reported that the trustees of Bethel Academy had directed this board to convey the lot formerly used as a common school, and recently sold to the trustees of Bethel Academy, to John L. Logan and Emma W. Logan for a consideration of fifteen hundred dollars ($1,500) and five hundred dollars ($500) due September 1st, 1893, and one thousand dollars ($1,000) due September 1st, 1894, with interest of seven percent from September 1st, 1893, until paid.

Appendix A-14
Deed between town of Nicholasville and the Logans
August 5, 1893

This deed between the Board of Councilmen of the town of Nicholasville (ex officio Trustees of Common School District No. 1 White in the County of Jessamine and the State of Kentucky partt of the first part) and John L. Logan and Emma W. Logan of the County and State aforesaid parties of the second part.

Witnesseth, that the said party of the first part, in consideration of the sum of fifteen hundred dollars, evidenced by two promissary notes of even date, hereof executed by the second parties payable to the trustees of Bethel Academy, one for five hundred dollars payable Sept. 1, 1893, and the other for one thousand dollars payable Sept. 1, 1894, with interest thereon at the rate of seven percent annum from the first day of September 1893 until paid and which notes are unpaid and to secure their payment a lien is retained on the property hereby conveyed, do hereby sell, grant and convey to the party of the second parties, their heirs and assigns, the following described being situated in Nicholasville, Jessamine County, on the west side of Seminary Street and bounded as follows: beginning at a point on Seminary Street corner tot he lot of David Moffat, thence south with said street one hundred and fifty feet to a stone corner to E.B. Hoovers lot, thence in a westerly direction parallel with Broadway Street to a stake in the east line of Bethel Academy ot, thence northerly with said line to a stake corner to David Moffats lot, thence easterly with his lot to the beginning, to have and to hold the same with all rights, privileges and appurtenances thereunto belonging or in any wise appertaining, unto said John Logan and Emma W. Logan and survivors of them and his or her heirs and assigns forever, with covenant of General Warranty.

Witness, its hands and seal this 5th day of August, 1893
The Board of Councilmen of the town of Nicholasville
by J.S. Bronaugh, Mayor

State of Kentucky, County of Jessamine

I, S. Perry, Clerk of the County Court of the County aforesaid, do certify that the foregoing instrument of writing from the Board of Councilmen of the town of Nicholasville to John L. Logan and Emma Logan were this day produced to me in my office, and were acknowledged by J.S. Bronaugh, Mayor, to be the act and deed of the Board of Councilmen of the town of Nicholasville, party thereto, and was lodged for record by the grantee, which together with this certificate, is duly recorded in my said office.

Given under my hand this 5th day of August, 1893
R.S. Perry, CJCC

APPENDIX B

APPENDIX B-1
An Act establishing Bethel Academy, and incorporating the Trustees thereof.
Approved February 10, 1798
Acts of 1798-1799-1800-1801. vol. 11, pp. 174-175.

Bethel Academy:

Section 1: Be it enacted by the General Assembly, that the Reverend Francis Poythress, John Knobler, Nathaniel Harris, John Metcalf, Barnabas M'Henry, James Crutcher, James Hord and Richard Masterson, shall be and they are hereby constituted a body politic and corporate, to be known by the name of Trustees of Bethel Academy, and by that name shall have perpetual succession, and a common seal, with power to change the same at pleasure; and as such shall be authorized to execute all powers and privileges that are enjoyed by trustees, governors or visitors of any college or university within this state, not herein limited or otherwise directed.

Section 2: The said trustees, or a majority of them, shall hold two stated, annual sessions in a year, or more, if to them it should seem necessary, at said academy.

Section 3: The said trustees and their successors, by the name aforesaid, shall be capable in law to purchase, receive and hold, to them and their successors, any lands, tenements, goods and chattels, of what kind soever, which shall be given or devised to, or purchased by them for the use of the said academy, and shall sell and dispose of the same in such manner as shall seem most conducive to the interest of the said academy.

Section 4: The said trustees may sue or be sued, plead or be impleaded, in any court of law or equity.

Section 5: they shall have power, from time to time, to establish such by-laws, rules and ordinances, not contrary to the constitution or laws of this commonwealth, as they shall deem necessary for the government of the said academy, and form general rules by which it may be determined when any trustee shall have vacated his seat.

Section 6: The president of said academy shall be a man of the most approved abilities in literature.

Section 7: The trustees shall elect their president, treasurer and clerk, and so many professors, tutors or masters as may be necessary; and upon the death, resignation or legal disability of any of the said trustees, president, or other officers of the said academy, or any removal from office, the board of trustees shall, by appointment, supply the vacancy occasioned thereby; and all trustees and officers of said academy, shall be elected by ballot.

Section 8: The chairman of the trustees shall have power to call a meeting of the trustees, and it shall be his duty, on the request of any three of them, to do the same, whenever cases of emergency require it; but upon any called meeting the chairman shall give at least ten days notice from the date of his circular letter or publication of said meeting, and the business that required the call shall be communicated and particularly specified.

Section 9: A majority of the whole number present, shall decide any question, motion, resolution or appointment.

Section 10: The treasurer, clerk and other subordinate officers, shall be subject to the direction of the board. This act shall commence and be in force from and after the passage thereof.

APPENDIX B-2
An Act of Endowment of Certain Seminaries of Learning, and for Other Purposes
Legislature of Commonwealth of Kentucky
Approved February 10, 1798

Section 1: Be it enacted by the General Assembly, that there shall be granted to the trustees of Kentucky, Franklin and Salem academies the following quantities of lands, that is to say, to the Kentucky academy, six thousand acres; to the Franklin academy, six thousand acres; to the Salem academy, six thousand acres; and the Bethel Academy, six thousand acres.

Section 2: And the trustees of the said academies for the time being, are hereby authorized and empowered, by themselves or agents, within ten months from the passage of this act, to cause to be surveyed the quantity of land hereby allowed to each academy on any vacant and unappropriated land within this state, on the south side of Green river, each quantity to be laid off in not more than twelve surveys, and no survey to be more than twice as long as wide; and shall moreover cause a platt and certificate of each survey to be returned to the surveyor's office of the county in which such survey may be, to be recorded, and the same shall be returned to the register's office of this state, and the register, without any fee, shall issue grants as in other cases. And the lands so patented shall be vested in the trustees of each academy respectively and their successors for ever; and the lands shall be free from taxes so long as they shall remain the property of said seminaries.

Section 3: And be it further enacted, that six thousand acres of land be and is hereby vested in Adam Rankin, Peter January, David Logan, William Robinson, David M'Gee, Richard Steele and James Scott, and their successors for ever, in trust for the use and benefit of the Lexington Seminary; also six thousand acres for the use and benefit of the Jefferson Seminary, to be vested in John Thompson, William Croghan, Alexander S. Bullitt, James Meriwether, John Thurston, Henry Churchill, William Taylor and Richard Clough Anderson, or a majority of them and their successors for ever, in trust for the benefit of the same, and said land to be entered, surveyed an patented by the said trustees, in the manner directed in the cases of the other academies in this act mentioned; and the said trustees and their successors for ever, shall be vested with similar powers over the same.

Section 4: The said trustees shall have power from time to time to fill any vacancies which may happen in their own body, and shall in all respects whatsoever, so far as the cases will apply, be governed by as enlarged rules and regulations, and be invested with as ample power and authority, as the trustees of either of the aforesaid academies are by this and any other act invested.

Section 5: It shall be lawful for the trustees of either of the said academies or seminaries, to sell one-third of the lands herby granted to the said academies and seminaries, and no more, without the future consent of the legislature, for the purpose of erecting their public buildings, purchasing a library and philosophical apparatus, provided that the lands hereby granted shall not be surveyed on any lands set apart for any Indian tribe.

Provided however, that no saltlick or spring, nor any bank, bed or pit of mine or ore of any valuable metal or mineral with one thousand acres, including the same, as near the center of a square as prior claims will admit of, shall be taken into any survey of land hereby granted.

And, whereas it is certain that however particular forms of government are better calculated than others to protect individuals in the free exercise of their natural rights, and are at the same time themselves better guarded against degeneracy, yet experience hath shewn that even under the best forms, those entrusted with power have in time and slow operation perverted it into tyranny, and it is believed that the most effectual means of preventing this, would be to illuminate, as far as possible the minds of the people at large, and more especially to give them knowledge of those facts which history exibiteth, that, possessed thereby of the experience of other ages and countries, they may be enabled to know ambition under all its shapes, and prompt to exert their natural powers to defeat its purposes; and whereas it is generally true, that people will be happier whose laws are best, and best administered, and that laws will be wisely formed and honestly administered in proportion as those who form and administer them are wise and hones, whence it becomes expedient, for promoting the public happiness, that those persons whom nature hath endowed with genius and virtue, should be rendered by liberal education, worthy to receive and able to guard the sacred deposit of the rights and liberties of their fellow citizens; and that to aid and accelerate this most desirable purpose, must be one of the first duties of every wise government.

Section 6: Be it therefore enacted by the General Assembly, that all the lands lying within the bounds of this commonwealth, on the south side of Cumberland River, below Obey's River, which is now vacant and unappropriated, or on which there shall not be, at the passage of this act, any actual settler under the laws of this state for the relief of settlers south of Green River, shall be and the same are hereby reserved by the General Assembly, to be appropriated as they may hereafter from time to time think fit, to the use of the seminaries of learning throughout the different parts of this commonwealth; and no person or persons shall after one month subsequent to the passage of this act, be permitted to settle on or take up any vacant land on the south side of Cumberland River as aforesaid, until the further order of the legislature; any law or laws to the contrary notwithstanding.

Note: the survey and patents of five plats totaling 4,935 acres are at the ofice of the Secretary of State and the Kentucky State Library and Archives in Frankfort, Kentucky. This land was located in what is now known as Henderson County. Before 1800 part of Henderson County was within the boundaries of Christian County.

APPENDIX B-3

An Act Authorizing the trustees of Bethel and Selby Academies to sell their lands, and for other purposes
Legislature of the Commonwealth of Kentucky
Approved January 30, 1810

Section 1: Be it enacted by the General Assembly, that the trustees of Bethel Academy may dispose of all the lands granted to them by this commonwealth, or such other lands and tenements they have by grant, or by other deed or deeds; and the trustees are hereby authorized and empowered to make deeds or conveyance for all or any part of the lands granted to them, by the name of the trustees of Bethel academy; either for cash in hand or on credit, or exchange them for other lands, for the only proper use and benefit of an institution of learning, either at the present site, in the county of Jessamine, or at any other place in the said county, a majority of the said trustees may direct; provided however, that the said trustees, or a mjority of them, may make use of so much of the proceeds of the sale of said lands as will be sufficient to reimburse them the expenses they may be at for the purpose of disposing of said lands, and purchasing other lands for the use of a public school in the said county of Jessamine.

Section 2: And be it further enacted, that the said trustees in their names may sue and be sued, and are hereby empowered to recover any monies now due them, or which may hereafter become due, for the sale of all or any part of the lands which in this act they are authorized to sell; and they are further empowered to purchase bank stock in the state bank to any amount not exceeding three fourths of the net proceeds of the sales of the lands now belonging to the Bethel Academy, and the interest arising from such stock shall be disposed in any manner that a majority of the said trustees or their successors may deem most to the advantage of the institution of learning, they have or may hereafter have in the county aforesaid.

Section 3: And be it further enacted, that the trustees of the Selby academy shall be and they are hereby authorized to sell the whole or such part of the land belonging to said academy as they shall think fit, for the purpose of completing the said academy and purchasing a library and globes; and the said trustees and their successors are hereby vested with full and complete power to convey to the purchaser the land by them sold for the purpose aforesaid.

APPENDIX B-4

Legislative Act of Kentucky Regarding Seminaries
Acts of 1815, pp. 269-271
Chap. CXCIII

An act authorizing the sale of seminary lands, and the investiture of the proceeds to bank stock.

Section 1: Be it enacted by the General Assembly of the Commonwealth of Kentucky, that the trustees of the seminaries in the several counties of this Commonwealth may, and they are hereby authorized to sell and convey to the respective purchasers thereof, all the lands with which they have been respectively endowed by the legislature of Kentucky.

Section 2: Be it further enacted, that the monies arising from sales of the said lands shall, by the said trustees, be vested in stock in the Bank of Kentucky, which stock, when purchased, shall belong to said seminaries respectively, by whose monies it was procured: the dividends and proceeds of which stock, may, from time to time be applied by trustees of the seminary to which it belongs, to procurement of more stock, until the annual proceeds or dividend thereof, shall amount to one thousand dollars; provided however, that where the majority of the trustees of any seminary, shall desire to erect the necessary buildings for the use and benefit of their seminary, it shall and may be lawful for said trustees to apply one fourth of the proceeds of the sale of their lands towards erection of said building.

Section 3: Be it further enacted, that when the stock of each seminary shall produce annually a dividend amounting to the aforesaid sum of one thousand dollars, the trustees thereof may, instead of accumulating stock by the application of the dividend thereto, apply the said dividend to the uses of the said seminary, or to the still further increase of stock, at their discretion and the state of the institution shall dictate.

Section 4: Be it further enacted, that the trustees of the aforesaid seminaries shall be allowed respectively, six percent, upon the money for which they shall have sold the lands aforesaid, for their trouble in selling the said lands and purchasing the bank stock as aforesaid; which six percent, they may respectively retain out of any dividends of said stock.

Section 5: Be it further enacted, that the trustees of each seminary, when they shall have sold the lands thereof, and vested the proceeds as aforesaid in bank stock, shall make out a report in writing of the quantity of land sold, of the price for which it was sold, of the person or persons to whom it was sold, of the county in which, and the watercourse upon it laid, of the number of shares of bank stock purchased; which said report shall be lodged with the clerk of the county court and carefully filed away and preserved by him, subject to the inspection of those whose interest or duty it may be to be informed of its contents.

Section 6: Be it further enacted, that the justices of the county courts of Allen and

Davies counties be, and they are hereby authorized to appropriate six thousand acres of land for the benefit of a seminary of learning, in each of their respective counties; subject, however, to the same laws and regulations now in force respecting the appropriation of seminary lands; and that they have two years allowed them from the passage of this act, for the appropriation of the same.

APPENDIX B-5

An Act to further regulate the Greenville and Bethel Seminaries.
Approved February 1, 1817
Acts of 1816, pp. 126-127

Bethel Seminary:

Section 2: Be it further enacted, that the trustees of Bethel Academy be, and they are hereby authorized to appropriate the sun of eight hundred dollars for the purchase of a suitable lot of ground in or near the town of Nicholasville, for the use of the said academy, the title of which shall be conveyed to and vest in the trustees and their successors for the purpose aforesaid.

APPENDIX B-6

Legislative Act of Kentucky Regarding Two Academies
Acts of 1819, p. 711
Chap. CCCXCV

An Act for the benefit of Bethel and Bourbon Academies.
Approved February 6, 1819

Be it enacted by the General Assembly of the Commonwealth of Kentucky, that so much of the act approved the 26th day of January, 1815, as authorizes the investment of the proceeds of sales of seminary lands in bank stock, be, and the same is hereby repealed, so far as it relates to the trustees of the Bethel and Bourbon academies; and the said trustees of said academies, respectively, are hereby authorized to appropriate the monies arising from the sales of any lands of said academies to the erection of the necessary buildings and improvements for the use of their respective academies.

APPENDIX B-7

Acts Establishing Academies in the State of Kentucky
Acts of 1857-1858. vol II, page 201
An act to amend an act, entitled, "an act to incorporate Bethel Academy."
Approved February 15, 1858

Bethel Academy:

Be it enacted by the General Assembly of the Commonwealth of Kentucky:

Section 1: That so much of the 1st section of an act establishing Bethel Academy, as relates to Trustees, and the manner of their election, be and the same is hereby so amended as to authorize the election of Trustees for said Academy, by the qualified voters of Jessamine county.

Section 2: There shall be one Trustee elected by the qualified voters of each voting precinct in said county, on the first Monday in August 1858, whose term of service shall be six years, unless vacated by death, removal, or resignation, in which event the majority of said Trustees may fill the vacancy so created, by the appointment of a suitable person from the district in which such vacancy occurs.

Section 3: The trustees of said Academy shall elect from their number a President, with such qualifications as are required by the 6th section of the original charter; they shall also elect a treasurer, who shall be required to give bond with approved security, for the faithful performance of his duties; they may also appoint a clerk, whose duty it shall be to keep a faithful record of the action of said Trustees from time to time.

Section 4: The trustees may have the privilege of sending to any school which may be taught at Bethel Academy a beneficiary pupil, who may be selected by said Trustees from the several precincts in the county: Provided, that if said pupil selected is not in a condition to pay for his tuition, then the tuition of said beneficiary may be appropriated out of the interest of any moneys which may be under the control of said Trustees.

Section 5: All provisions in the original act of incorporation not in conflict with this amendment, shall remain in full force; and any other act or acts which may conflict with the provisions of this amendment are hereby repealed.

Section 6: The election of said Trustees shall be governed by the rules that govern the general elections of this Commonwealth.

Section 7: This act shall take effect from and after its passage.

(Under Bourbon Academy see act entitled Bourbon and Bethel Academies, Jan. 6, 1819).

APPENDIX B-8

Acts establishing academies in the state of Kentucky
Acts of 1863-1864, p. 375
An act to repeal an act, entitled, an act to amend an act, entitled, an act to incorporate Bethel Academy.
Approved February 13, 1864.

Bethel Academy:

Be it enacted by the General Assembly of the Commonwealth of Kentucky:

Section 1: That an act, entitled, and act to amend an act, entitled, an act to incorporate Bethel Academy, approved the 15th day of February, 1858, be and the same is hereby repealed.

Section 2: That instead of the persons mentioned in the first section of an act, entitled, an act establishing Bethel Academy, and incorporating the trustees thereof, approved the 10th day of February, 1798, the following named persons shall be and they are hereby constituted and appointed the corporators and trustees of Bethel Academy, to-wit: George

Brown, John S. Bronaugh, Isaac Barkley, Newton Dickerson, Moreau Brown, Lewis H. Chrisman, and Thos. Crutcher; and said corporators and trustees, and their successors in office, be and they are hereby invested with all the rights, privileges, and immunities that were conferred upon the original corporators and trustees by the said act of incorporation, and the several amendatory acts thereto.

Section 3: This act shall take effect and be in force from and after the first day of July next.

APPENDIX B-9

An Act for the benefit of Bethel Academy, in the county of Jessamine.
Approved April 16, 1873
Acts of 1873, vol. 11, p. 315

Bethel Academy:

Be it enacted by the General Assembly of the Commonwealth of Kentucky:

Section 1: That the board of trustees of Bethel Academy, in Jessamine County, shall have power to lease or sell the property held by them for educational purposes to the trustees of common schools in district no. 1, embracing the town of Nicholasville, in said county.

Section 2: That the proceeds arising from the sale or lease of said academy shall be paid to the common school commissioner by the trustees of said academy; and said commissioner shall pay to the trustees of each district in the county an equal share of said proceeds, to be used in aid of the common school of said district severally.

Section 3: That this act shall take effect from its passage.

Appendix C

APPENDIX C-1

The trustees of Bethel Academy being authorized by the legislature of Kentucky to dispose of their donation LANDS, do offer the following tracts for sale; viz.—

2,780 acres

On the Ohio river, opposite the mouth of the Saline creek.

1,600 acres

In two surveys, adjoining Col. Waggoner's

755 acres

Adjoining Maj. Fielding Jones. All those lands lie near together, and are valuable. They will be sold together, or in separate tracts—several valuable farms on them, a small part of the purchase money will be required in hand, the balance in 6 annual installments. For further particulars, apply to Nathaniel Harris and Maddox Fisher, in Lexington, Ky. 6in.

APPENDIX C-2

Nicholasville Bethel Academy
Summer Session

The undersigned having lately located in the town of Nicholasville, and taken charge of Bethel Academy, would respectfully announce to the citizens of the town and county generally, that he will open his Summer Session on Monday, May 15th.

Having taught in Jessamine and several of the adjoining counties, he is willing to give references for attention to business, and success in the progress of scholars under his care to all persons who have patronized him heretofore, and pledges himself to use every effort in his power to give entire satisfaction to all who may favor him with their patronage again.

The society in and around Nicholasville, is as moral, religious and peaceable, perhaps, as that of any other town in the state.

The site of the Academy is one of the most elevated and healthy in the place, in a secluded spot, separate and apart from the hum and business of the town, where there is nothing to interrupt the student in the prosecution of his studies.

Boarding can be had upon reasonable terms in the town and vicinity, at a

convenient distance from the Academy.
    Terms of Session 22 weeks.
M. Hagen, Principal.
Nicholasville, Ky.
Lexington Observer & Reporter
May 10, 1848, page 3, col.7 (advertisement)

APPENDIX C-3

Bethel Academy
Nicholasville, Kentucky
Marriage of Mr. John F. Metcalf—Mr. Metcalf is the grandson of Rev. John Metcalf—
He was also the first teacher in Bethel Academy in 1794.
Lexington Daily Press April 11, 1882, p. 4, col. 3

Old Bethel Academy
Her Teachers and Traditions
Nicholasville, Ky., May 5, 1882

    In one of our town papers, The School Boy, of April 26, I have read a brief historic
notice of Bethel Academy, with the above heading and signed "The School-boys Friend." I
have facts to prove that the Rev. John Metcalf was the first Principal, who took charge of
Bethel Academy in January 1794. the Academy was first founded in 1790, two years before
Kentucky became a sovereign state. I have also in my possession several old MSS. and
other documentary evidence to show that the Academy was not open for reception of
pupils until the Rev. John Metcalf first took charge as Principal in the year 1794. When the
poor "toady" who wrote the article signed "The School-boys Friend" was invited to write
up the history of Old Bethel Academy he requested me to give him some facts concerning
the early history of Old Bethel, her fist teachers, etc. I showed him an autograph letter of
John Metcalf, dated January 15, 1794, addressed to Hon. George Nicholas, in which he
states, "I have been so confined for the last two weeks in fitting up suitable places of abode
for some of my pupils that I have greatly neglected my private affairs." In 1796 he gave up
the Academy to Francis Poythress, whose health compelled him to leave the Lexington
Circuit. Poythress gave the school up in 1797, and was succeeded by Valentine Cook, who
was induced to take charge of the school in 1799. Mr. Cook continued the school three
years, and was succeeded by Rev. Nathaniel Harris, who was Principal of the English
department in the Academy at the time Valentine Cook took charge of it in 1799. It was in
1805 that the Academy was removed to Nicholasville, and John Metcalf again assumed the
duties as principal of Bethel Academy, and so continued up to the time of his death, which
was in 1820. When I furnish facts to a man to write I hope hereafter he may see and make
better use of them than the gentleman who signs himself "The Schoolboy's Friend."
    S.M. Duncan.
    The Lexington Daily Press, May 6, 1882, p. 4, col. 3

APPENDIX C-4

Bethel Academy
Nicholasville, Kentucky
An English and Classical High School
A.N. Gordon, Principal, J.L. Logan, Assistant
Session of 1877-78

Location

In natural beauty of location, Bethel Academy can hardly be surpassed by any school in the central part of the state. It is situated upon a rising ground at the western limit of the town of Nicholasville, Jessamine Co., Ky., and commands an extensive view in every direction of the rich and highly cultivated lands around. When properly laid out and improved (which the Principal hopes will be done before a great while), there will not be a more beautiful "five acres" in the whole Blue Grass country.

The town is high and healthful, and the people, as a class, moral and industrious.

Aims of the school

Having leased this property for a term of years, the Principal proposes to build up a High-School in the truest sense of the term—a school where young men may be fitted for discharging the ordinary duties of life with intelligence and success, and where boys may be prepared to enter advanced classes in our best colleges.

Constant drill will be a characteristic of the school, and thoroughness in every department will be insisted upon.

Organization

The School is divided into two Departments, High-School and Preparatory. The Preparatory Department has been added, in order that the Principal may have boys in preparation, under his own supervision, for positions in his higher classes. It will include such studies as are required to be taught in our common Schools. The High-School Department will embrace those studies usually pursued during the first two or three years at college.

The principal has secured the assistance of Mr. John Lewis Logan, of Virginia, a graduate of Washington and Lee University and medalist in the departments of Latin, Greek and Mathematics. Mr. Logan has taught with success for the last five or six years, and the Principal considers himself fortunate in being able to associate so good a teacher with himself in the work of the school.

The school-rooms will be thoroughly renovated and supplied with new and improved furniture.

Discipline

The School will be kept strictly select. None but those supposed to be gentlemen will be admitted; and should a pupil prove incorrigible, or his habits, in or out of school, be found to be corrupting, he will be required to discontinue his connection with the institution.

A high moral tone will be cultivated, and the pupils will be expected to govern themselves in all matters of importance. In minor matters the discipline will be gentle; but prompt and cheerful obedience, in every particular, will be expected.

Examinations

Rigid written examinations will be held, in the higher classes, at the close of the year, and at such other times as the Principal may think proper. The lower classes will be examined orally. All pupils will be required to attend these examinations.

Prizes

To encourage diligence and reward merit, several public-spirited gentlemen have offered a number of valuable prizes in the various studies as follows:

> To the pupil with highest standing in Languages, A Gold Medal, by Col. Bennett H. Young.
> To the pupil with highest standing in Mathematics, A Gold medal, by Col. Bennett H. Young.
> To the pupil with highest standing in Spelling, "The Poythress Prize in Spelling," A copy of **Worcester's Unabridged Dictionary**.
> To the pupil with highest standing in Reading and Elocution, a handsome prize.

Terms (Per session of forty weeks),
Payable, one-third in advance, one-third at Christmas, and one-third at the end of the session:

High-School Department	$60.00
Preparatory Department	50.00
Incidental Fee, (in advance)	2.50

Pupils entering before Christmas will be charged for the whole session; those entering after that time will be charged for a half session, but payment will be required in advance.

Pupils entering at any time during the year will pay the whole incidental fee.

No deduction will be made for absence, except in cases of protracted sickness.

The above terms will be invariably adhered to, and patrons of the School are requested not to ask a deviation in their favor; but where it is not convenient to pay on the day stipulated, a 30-days' note, with approved security, negotiable and payable in bank, will be received as cash.

Board can be had in good families at moderate rates.

APPENDIX C-5

Bethel Academy
Session of 1878-79

History

Bethel Academy is the oldest institution for intermediate instruction in the State of

Kentucky. It was founded by the Kentucky Conference of the Methodist Episcopal Church in the year 1790, at a time when its solid walls were required not only to furnish a shelter from the elements and supply instruction, but to offer a fortification against the attacks of the Indians. It was picturesquely located upon a high bluff overlooking the Kentucky river, on what was then the main thoroughfare for the emigrants from Virginia to the "Dark and Bloody Ground." For a number of years it prospered under the management of its founders, but afterwards, for some unexplained causes, it gradually declined, until, finally, it passed entirely from the control of the M.E. Church to a non-sectarian Board of Trustees, who hold it in trust for higher education in Kentucky.

The location having been found unfavorable for the prosperity of the school, it was changed, and Nicholasville selected—the brick from the old house having been hauled and put into the new.

Thus we see that Bethel Academy has a history as old as the State, tradition even claiming that it had an embryonic existence while Kentucky was still a county in Virginia.

Charter

In 1798 the General Assembly granted a most liberal charter to this institution, bestowing upon it privileges as extensive as those of any institution in the State.

This charter is still in force, and offers to the people of Jessamine county a basis upon which they can and ought to build up a Collegiate High School which would carry out the hopes of its original founders, be an honor to themselves, and command patronage from the whole State, and even from other States.

Location

In natural beauty the present location of Bethel Academy can hardly be surpassed by that of any school in the central portion of the State. It is situated upon a rising ground at the western limit of the town of Nicholasville, and commands an extensive view, in almost every direction, of the rich and highly cultivated lands around.

Nicholasville is twelve miles south of Lexington, on the Cincinnati Southern Railway, in the centre of a refined and prosperous community, and is, withal, exceptionally healthful. No fatal disease, so far as known, has ever been contracted by pupils attending this school, and the Principal believes that parents and guardians (especially in the South), can put their boys in no more healthful community.

Aims of the School

Having leased this property for a term of years, the Principal proposes to build up, and maintain, a High School in the truest sense of the term, a school where young men may fit themselves for entering advanced classes in our best colleges, or where those not having a college course in view may get such mental training as will enable them to grapple successfully with the questions presenting themselves in whatever business they may choose to follow.

Methods

Our purpose will be so to instruct as to make the pupils think for themselves, avoiding the common error of cramming the mind with a mass of facts which, by reason and reflection, the pupil does not make his own. Thoroughness, therefore, rather than rapidity of progress, will be aimed at. With this object in view, the pupil will be required to master the subject in hand before passing to the higher studies of the course.

The morals and manners of the pupils will be diligently guarded, as it is the anxious desire of the Principal that the boys in his school be educated into noble, Christian gentlemen.

Discipline

The school is, and will be kept, strictly select. None but those supposed to be gentlemen will be admitted; and should a pupil prove incorrigible, or his habits, in or out of school, be found to be corrupting, he will be required to withdraw. Few rules of conduct will be laid down, but such deportment as is proper in a refined Christian family will be expected.

Pupils are put upon their honor, and treated as gentlemen, yet mild but firm discipline will be exercised in minor matters, and a prompt and cheerful obedience, in every particular, will be expected.

Pupils will be understood to pledge themselves, by the very act of entering the school, to observe all the rules of the school, and especially to abstain from the use of all intoxicating liquors, and from having in their possession, or under their control, an deadly weapon, while in attendance upon the sessions of the school.

Prizes

To encourage diligence and reward merit, several public spirited gentlemen have offered a number of valuable prizes in the several studies as follows:

> To the pupil with highest standing in languages, a Gold Medal, by Col. Bennett H. Young.
> To the pupil with highest standing in Mathematics, A Gold Medal, by Col. Bennett H. Young.
> To the pupil with highest standing in spelling, "The Poythress Prize in Spelling," a copy of Worcester's Unabridged Dictionary, by a gentleman of Nicholasville.
> To the pupil in the High School Department with highest standing in Reading and Elocution, a handsome prize by the Principal.
> To the pupil in Preparatory Department, with highest standing in Reading and Elocution, a handsome prize, by a lady of Nicholasville.

These prizes will be publicly conferred at the closing exercises in June.
Recipients of prizes for session of 1877-78.

Bennett H. Young, Medal in Mathematics—Thomas R. Welch.
Bennett H. Young, Medal in Languages—George A.A.C. Hutchison.
Prize in Reading and Elocution—Robert G. Lowrey.
"Poythress Prize in Spelling"—William Rice Harris.

Recipients of Prizes for session of 1878-79.
    Bennett H. Young Medal in Mathematics—Levi Pearce.
    Bennett H. Young, Medal in Languages—Levi Pearce.
    Prize in Reading and Elocution, Samuel E. Davis.
    "Poythress Prize in spelling," Geo. A.C. Hutchison.

Terms per session of forty weeks

Payable, one-third in advance, one-third at Christmas, and one-third at the end of the session.

High-School Department	$60.00
Preparatory Department	50.00
Incidental Fee (in advance)	2.50

Pupils entering before Christmas will be charged for the whole session; those entering after that time will be charged for a half session, but payment will be required in advance.

Pupils entering at any time during the year will pay the whole incidental fee. No deduction will be made for absence, except in cases of protracted sickness.

The above terms will be invariable adhered to, and patrons of the school are requested not to ask a deviation in their favor.

Board can be had in good families at from $3.00 to $4.00 per week, exclusive of washing.

References

The Principal takes the liberty of referring to the following gentlemen, most of whom have been patrons, and have known both Mr. Logan and himself as teachers. He craves the indulgence of these gentlemen for referring to them without consultation with them.

The Board of Trustees, and other patrons, at and around Nicholasville, Ky.

Gen. G.W.C. Lee, President of Washington and Lee University, Lexington, Va., and other members of the faculty of that institution.

Gen. F.H. Smith, Superintendent Virginia Military Institute, Lexington, Va.

Col. J.T.L. Preston, of same institution.

Col. Bennett H. Young, of Louisville, Ky.

Dr. John W. Pratt, President of Central University, Richmond, Ky.

Prof. W.H. Stuart, Shelbyville, Ky.

Rev. G.H. Route, Versailles, Ky.

Rev. R.H. Kinnaird, Midway, Ky.

Rev. R. Cecil, Mercer County, Ky.

Hon. H.L. Stone, Mt. Sterling, Ky.

Personal

In sending out this annual catalogue, the Principal would take occasion to thank his patrons for their generous and hearty support, and he will "do his endeavors" to deserve a continuance of their confidence and patronage in the future.

It is with real gratification that he announces the return of Mr. Logan, as his assistant for another year. He does not know a more competent, conscientious, and pains-taking teacher in the range of his acquaintance, and he believes that Mr. Logan's work is telling for good on the school.

Calendar
Session begins September 1st, 1879.
Adjourns for Christmas Holidays, December 24.
Resumes work January 5th, 1880.
Final examinations begin May 25th, 1880.
Closing exercises, June 5th, 1880.

APPENDIX C-6

Bethel Academy: An English and Classical High School for Boys
A.N. Gordon, Principal
Session of 1878-79

Announcement

Prizes
> To encourage diligence and reward merit, the following prizes are offered:
> To the pupil with highest standing in languages, a Gold Medal, by Col. Bennett H. Young.
> To the pupil with highest standing in Mathematics, a Gold Medal, by Col. Bennett H. Young.
> To the pupil who has completed the High School Department with highest average in Latin, Greek and Mathematics, a scholarship for one year in Central University.
> To the pupil with the highest standing in spelling, "The Poythress Prize in Spelling," a copy of Worcester's Unabridged Dictionary, by a gentleman of Nicholasville.
> To the pupil in High School Department with highest standing in the English course, a handsome prize by the principal.
> To the pupil in the Primary Department with highest standing in the English course, a handsome prize.
> No prize will be awarded to any pupil whose standing and deportment does not merit it.

Bethel Academy
This school aims at thorough ground-work in all departments; and the uniformly high stand taken by its pupils in all the colleges attended by them is referred to as proof of the efficiency of the instruction

High-toned manliness in thought and action, coupled with gentle manners, and, above all, pure morals, are carefully inculcated, and, it is hoped, exemplified. The pupil is put upon his honor and taught the value of personal integrity and trustworthiness; while at the same time a ready obedience to authority, a careful preparation of his studies, and a prompt discharge of every duty is firmly insisted on.

The principal, while returning his thanks for the patronage and support of past years, invites those who approve of the aims and methods of the school, and who desire their sons to undergo its discipline and training, to give it their patronage and support for the year to come.

APPENDIX C-7

1883 Advertisement

Bethel Academy

A Home School For boys and Young Men, where they may fit themselves for business life, or for advanced classes in our best colleges and universities.

The pupils trained at Bethel Academy, under the present management, have always taken the very highest stand in their classes at college, and have carried off their full share of medals and distinctions.

The next session begins September 3, 1883, and continues forty weeks, including Christmas. Mr. G.A.C. Hutchison will assist the Principal the next year.

Terms per annual session,

Payable, one-third in advance, one-third at Christmas, and one-third the end of the session:

Primary Department	$40.00
Preparatory Department	50.00
High School Department	60.00
Incidental fees	2.50

Pupils entering before Christmas will be charged for the whole session; those entering after that time will be charged for a half session, but payment will be required in advance.

Pupils entering at any time during the year will pay the whole incidental fee.

No deduction will be made for absence, except in cases of protracted sickness.

The above terms will be invariably adhered to, and patrons of the school are requested not to ask a deviation in their favor.

Board can be had in good families at from $3.00 to $4.00 per week, exclusive of washing.

For further information apply to A.N. Gordon, Principal, Nicholasville, Ky.

APPENDIX C-8

Anniversary Dinner

Given in celebration of the seventy-fifth birthday of A.N. Gordon, teacher, by his pupils, July first, nineteen hundred and twenty-two, six thirty p.m., Phoenix Hotel.

Teacher

Mr. Gordon taught school for forty-seven years from 1866 to 1913. He was principal of the schools in which he taught, except at Shelbyville and Richmond.

To His Old Pupils

> *The Lord bless you and keep you;*
> *The Lord make his face to shine upon you*
> *and be gracious unto you;*
> *The Lord lift up his countenance upon you and give you PEACE.*
> — *Num. VI, 24-26.*

Mr. Gordon taught at the times and places named below:

Pekin, (Jessamine County) Kentucky	Fall of 1866
Owingsville, (Bath County) Kentucky	1868-69
Lexington, Virginia	1870-71
Shelbyville, Kentucky	1873-74
Central University, Richmond, Kentucky	1874-76
Nicholasville, Kentucky	1876-87
"Alleghan," (Fayette County) Kentucky	1887-1900
Lexington, Kentucky	1900-05
"Glen Airy," near Frankfort, Kentucky	1905-08
Lexington, Kentucky	1909-1913

Program

Toast Master	Judge Richard C. Stoll
Invocation	Rev. D. Clay Lilly
"The Soldier"	Rev. E.L. Southgate
"The Citizen"	Mr. A.H. Jewell
"The Teacher"	Mr. Graddy Cary
"The Churchman"	Dr. F.H. Clarke
"Bethel Academy"	Mr. B.Y. Willis
Informal Remarks	Former Pupils

Menu

Chilled Cantaloupe, Radishes, Olives, Fillet of Sole with tartar sauce, Long Branch Potatoes, Roast Spring Chicken, Au Gratin Potatoes, Peas in Cream Sauce, Lettuce and Tomato Salad, Thousand Island Dressing, Apple pie a la mode, Coffee, Rolls

APPENDIX C-9
A Litany of Re-dedication for Bethel Academy
Founded by Bishop F. Asbury in 1790
World Methodist Historical Society, North American Sector Meeting
Asbury Theological Seminary, August 6-10, 1984

A Litany of Re-dedication

> **Leader:** Blessed art thou, Lord God of our fathers: Praised and exalted above all forever.

Congregation: Blessed art thou for the name of thy majesty: Praised and exalted above all forever.

Leader: Blessed art thou in the temple of thy holiness: Praised and exalted above all forever.

Congregation: Praise be to thee for thy servants our fathers: Who brought us thy name and thy word; Who taught us thy truth and thy love; Who journeyed through storm and flood, through sickness and suffering, through life and death.

Leader: To give us this house of God, named Bethel, to establish the foundations of a mighty heritage in Kentucky, To raise a symbol of everlasting grace to us who follow in their train.

Congregation: There are some of them who have left a name, so that men declare their praise.

Leader: And there are some who have no memorial, who have perished as though they had not lived.

Congregation: But these were men and women of mercy; whose righteous deeds have not been forgotten.

Leader: Their prosperity will remain with their descendents, and their inheritance to their children's children.

All: Their glory will not be blotted out. Blessed are thou O Lord, the God of Israel, our Father forever and ever.

APPENDIX C-10

Asbury College 1890-1990
Our Heritage
Seeking Knowledge • Serving Christ

A Service of Heritage Awareness and Dedication
of the Bethel Academy Historical Marker
October 7, 1988
Hughes Auditorium
10:00 a.m.

Program of Heritage Awareness

Prelude ....*Variations on a Chorale Theme* ....Johann G. Walther
Professor Gerard Faber, College Organist

Welcome ....Dr. Paul Vincent

Hymn.......................................*Faith of Our Fathers* ....Frederick W. Faber
Beatrice Hill Holz, Song Leader

Invocation ....Dr. Terry Faris
Pastor, Wilmore United Methodist Church

Scripture....................1Samuel 7:9-12, Deuteronomy 6:4-13 ....Dr. David Ditto
Member, Alumni Board of Directors
Anthem.......................................*Praise the Lord* ....James Curnow
Dr. Ronald W. Holz, trumpet
Professor Gerard Faber, organ
Message...........*Publish Your Message in the Open Face of the Sun*......Dr. Dennis Kinlaw
President, Asbury College

Service of Dedication

    Leader: It is right and proper that this historical marker should be formally and devoutly set apart as a memorial of the founding of Bethel Academy, Asbury College and Asbury Theological Seminary. For such a dedication we are now assembled. And, as the dedication of any building or monument is vain without the solemn consecration of those whose labor and interests it represents, let us now give ourselves anew to the service of God: our souls, that they may be renewed after the image of Christ; our bodies, that they may be fit temples for indwelling of the Holy Spirit; and our work and business, that they may be according to God's holy will, and that their fruit may lead to the glory of His name and the advancement of His kingdom.

    People: We, the faculty, administration, students, staff and friends of this college, compassed about with a great cloud of witnesses, grateful for our heritage, sensible of the sacrifice of our fathers in the faith do dedicate this marker as a lasting symbol and a perpetual reminder of the great providence of God in raising up and sustaining His work in our midst. As we do, we dedicate ourselves anew to the worship and service of Almighty God; through Jesus Christ our Lord. Amen.

    Leader: Hear the word of the Lord. And the children of Israel...took up twelve stones out of the midst of Jordan, as the Lord spake unto Joshua, according to the number of the tribes of the children of Israel, and carried them over with them unto the place where they lodged, and laid them down there. And Joshua set up twelve stones in the midst of Jordan, in the place where the feet of the priests which bare the ark of the covenant stood: and they are there unto this day. Joshua 4: 8-9

    Leader: Even as Joshua set up memorial stones on the banks of the Jordan, we rejoice in this memorial stone which by the favor of God and the labor of man has been established in this place.

(Dedication)

    Leader: We dedicate this marker...

    People: As a reminder of the miraculous founding and distinguished history of the academy, the college and the seminary.

    Leader: We dedicate this marker...

    People: As a reminder that God's ever faithful covenant love has attended the history, guided the leaders, and preserved the distinctive character and mission of these institutions under God.

Leader: We dedicate this marker…

People: As a reminder of the shared history and common story of Asbury College and Asbury Theological Seminary.

Leader: We dedicate this marker…

People: As a reminder to ourselves and to future generations that campus brick and mortar, wood and steel, things of time, are part of a kingdom God is building that will never pass away.

Leader: Let us pray. Almighty God, and heavenly Father, whose eyes are ever toward the righteous, and whose ears are ever open unto their cry: Graciously accept, we pray thee, this marker which we now dedicate to thee, for thy service and to thy glory; for those who may pause in its shadow and peruse its inscription, we pray that thy love and wisdom may unite to make plain the path of knowledge and service; and we beseech thee, receive us thy servants who here dedicate ourselves anew to thee and to those offices of fellowship and good will in which thou are well pleased. Grant that those who pass here, whether administrators, teachers, students or guests may come with pure minds, upright purpose, and steadfast endeavor to learn and do they holy will, through Jesus Christ our Lord. Amen.

Information on the Bethel Academy Historical Marker

Bethel Academy

This was second Methodist school in United States. In 1790 Bishop Francis Asbury laid plans for Bethel Academy, four miles southeast of Wilmore on cliffs above Kentucky River. It was operating by 1794, closed ca. 1804, due to lack of funds and Indian hostilities. Second site was in Nicholasville, 1820-93.

Asbury College

Established in 1890, this school was named for Francis Asbury first Methodist bishop and circuit rider in United States. Asbury Theological Seminary was established at Asbury College, 1923. Original Bethel Academy site and Asbury College Administration Building are listed on National Register of Historic Places.

BETHEL ACADEMY:
MORE IMPORTANT DOCUMENTS

—————•◦•◦•—————

GEORGE HERBERT LIVINGSTON

At the time my reports on Bethel Academy were published in *The Asbury Theological Journal*, vol. 49, no. 2, incomplete information was available about the 6,000 acres granted to Bethel Academy in 1798 by the General Assembly of the Commonwealth of Kentucky. The Act of Endowment is found reproduced on pp. 96-98 of the above mentioned *Journal* with a note at the end of it. This note has a factual error for the statement, "4,935 acres" for the total should have been 5,935 acres, and we now know that the parcels of land that made up this acreage are in Union County, which was formed from the western end of Henderson County in 1810.

The purpose of this article is to provide the text of the surveys and patents of the parcels of land that made up the endowment and maps of sections of Union County which show the location of the creeks mentioned in the documents. The secretary of the Union County Historical Society has informed me that bills of sale of these parcels of land are not now available because the deed book containing them is going through the process of microfilming and thus unavailable to the public. Hopefully, when the microfilms of the deed book are completed, the text of these bills of sale can be published.

There are five pairs of surveys and patents numbered: 3543, 3551, 3553, 5162 #2, and 5985. The documents each have a drawing of the parcel of land described. The surveys are kept in the Office of the Secretary of State, Commonwealth of Kentucky, Frankfort, Kentucky. Microfilms of the patents are kept in the Public Records Division, Department of Libraries and Archives in the same state and city.

This is the text of survey and patent number 3543:

Survey 3543
Surveyed for the Trustees of Bethel Academy: Francis Poythress, John Kobler,

---

George Herbert Livingston is professor emeritus of Old Testament at Asbury Theological Seminary in Wilmore, Kentucky.

Livingston

Nathaniel Harris, Barnabas M'Henry, James Croucher (correct spelling Crutcher),
James Howard (correct spelling Hord), John Metcalf, and Richard Masterson and
their successors, 2780 acres of land granted by the legislature of Kentucky to said
Trustees and their successors, lying in the county of Christian, on the Ohio River, to
wit: Beginning on the Bank of the River at three Hicory, Elm and Muberry, running
thence North 65 degrees E. 731 poles to a small Elm, Maple and Gum, thence
North 25 degrees West 711 poles to two Hicorys, a small Elm and Ash on a ridge,
thence South 58 degrees W. 777 poles to a water poplar on the Bank of the river,
thence down the Meanders and bending thereon S. 25 degrees E. 308 poles thence
South 30 degrees E. 324 poles to the beginning.

> Dan'l Ashley D.S.
> Surveyed June 20, 1798

Fielding Jones
John Buchannan
John Waggoner, M.
C. C.   Examined and recorded the 2nd July 1798
               Young Ewing S. C. C.

A map is top front of the document and these notations are on the back:

The Trustees of Bethel Academy 2780 Acres
Recorded and Examined N. 3543 5/404
Received 28th Nov. '98
Certified 28th June 1799
R in Bk 5, Page 404

Note: This record is now kept in the Office of the Secretary of State, of the State of
Kentucky in Frankfort, KY.

Patent # 3543
James Garrard Esquire Governor of the Commonwealth of Kentucky to all whom
these presents shall come greeting. Know ye that by virtue and in consideration of an
act of the Assembly passed the tenth day of February, 1798 entitled an act for the
endowment of certain Seminaries of learning and for other purposes there is granted
by the said Commonwealth unto Francis Poythress, John Kobler, Nathaniel Harris,
Barnabas M'Henry, James Croucher, James Howard, John Metcalf and Richard
Masterson, Trustees of Bethel Academy for the use and purpose as are proposed in
the aforesaid act a certain tract or parcel of land containing two thousand seven hundred and eighty acres by survey bearing date the twentieth day of January one thousand seven hundred and ninety eight lying and being in the County of Christian on
the Ohio River are bounded as followeth, to wit: beginning on the bank of the river
at three Hickories and Mulberry, running thence North sixty five degrees East seven
hundred and thirty-one poles to a small Elm, Maple and Gum, thence North twenty-

five degrees West seven hundred and eleven poles to two Hickories a small Elm and Ash on a ridge. Thence South fifty-eight degrees West seven hundred and seventy-seven poles to a water poplar on the bank of the river, thence down the meanders and bending thereon South twenty-five degrees East three hundred and eight poles thence South thirty degrees East three hundred and twenty four poles to the beginning with its appurtenances to have and to hold the said tract or parcel of land with its appurtenances to the said Francis Poythress etc. and their successors whereof the said James Garrard Esq. Governor of the Commonwealth of Kentucky hath hereto set his hand and causeth the seal of the said Commonwealth to be affixed at Frankfort on the twenty-eighth day of June in the year of our Lord one thousand and ninety-nine and of the Commonwealth the Eighth.

By the Governor   James Garrard
                              Harry Toulman, Sec't

Notation on left margin: Examined and Delivered to James Hord 2nd Aug '99.

The Following are the texts of the survey and patent of number 3551.

SURVEY 3551
Surveyed for Trustees of Bethel Academy: Francis Poythress, John Kobler, Nathaniel Harris, Barnabas M'Henry, James Croucher, James Howard, John Metcalf, and Richard Masterson, and their successors, 265 acres of land granted by the legislature of Kentucky to said Trustees and their successors, lying in the County of Christian on the waters of the Ohio, to wit: Beginning at a sweet Gum and Dogwood on the side of a ridge, running thence S. 21 degrees W. 260 poles to 2 white oakes crossing a small branch at 160 poles thence S. 69 degrees E. 170 poles to 2 black oakes, thence N. 21 degrees W. 260 poles to 3 black oakes on the side of a hill thence N. 69 degrees W. 170 poles to the beginning.

                                        Dan'l Ashley, D. S.
                                 Surveyed 22nd of June 1798

Fielding Jones
John Buchannan
John Waggoner, M.   Examined and recorded this 2nd July 1798 by
     C. C.   Young Ewing S. C. C.

Note: There is a map of the survey at the top of the front page and these notations on the back:

The Trustees of Bethel Academy 265 acres

Livingston

Recorded and examined #3551
Received 28th Nov. '98
Certified 25th June '99
Recorded in Book 5 Page 412

Note: This record is now kept in the Office of the Secretary of State, of the State of Kentucky in Frankfort, KY., and also on microfilm in the State Library and Archives, Frankfort, KY.

PATENT #3551

Secretary of State, Kentucky Land Office, Old Kentucky Grants
Book 11, pages 517-518.

James Garrard Esquire Governor of the Commonwealth of Kentucky to all to whom these presents shall come greetings. Know ye that by virtue and in consideration of an act of the Assembly passed the tenth day of February, 1798, entitled an act for the endowment of certain Seminaries of learning or other purposes there is granted by the said Commonwealth unto Francis Poythress, John Kobler, Nathaniel Harris, Barnabas M'Henry, James Croucher, James Howard, John Metcalf and Richard Masterson, Trustees of Bethel Academy for the use and purpose as are proposed in the aforesaid act a certain tract or parcel of land containing two hundred and sixty-five acres by survey bearing date twenty-second day of June one thousand seven hundred and ninety-eight lying and being in the County of Christian on the waters of the Ohio River bounded as followeth, to wit: Beginning at sweet Gum and Dogwood on the side of a ridge running thence South twenty-one degrees West two hundred and sixty poles to two White Oaks crossing a small Branch at the one hundred and sixty poles thence South sixty-nine degrees East one hundred and seventy poles to two Black Oaks thence North twenty one degrees East to two Black Oaks on the side of a hill thence North sixty-nine degrees West one hundred seventy poles to the Beginning with appurtenances to have and to hold the said tract or parcel of land with appurtenances to the said Francis Poythress use and their heirs forever. In witness whereof the said James Garrard Esquire Governor of the Commonwealth of Kentucky hath hereto set his hand and caused the seal of the said Commonwealth to be affixed at Frankfort on the twenty-eighth day of June in the year of our Lord one thousand and ninety-nine and of the Commonwealth of the Eighth.

By the Governor   James Garrard
                         Harry Toulman, Sec't

Notation on the left margin: Francis Poythress 265 acres
Christian County   N. 818
Delivered to James Hord 2nd Aug '99

Note that these two parcels of land border on the Ohio River.

SURVEY #3553

Surveyed for the Trustees of Bethel Academy: Francis Poythress, John Kobler, Nathaniel Harris, Barnabas M'Henry, James Croucher, James Howard, John Metcalf and Richard Masterson and their successors, 1090 acres of land granted by the legislature of Kentucky to said Trustees and their successors, lying in the County of Christian, on a branch of Lost Creek the waters of Ohio, to wit: Beginning at a poplar sugar tree and Black Gum running thence N. 21 degrees E. 43 poles to 2 Black Ashes and Hicory crossing a branch at 205 one at 236 poles, thence N. 20 degrees E. 80 poles to a Hicory, Black Ashe and White Oake in the head of a hollow, thence S. 70 degrees E. 420 poles to a sweet Gum and 2 poplars crossing a branch of Lost Creek several times at 140 poles, thence S. 21 degrees W. 252 poles to White Oake a Black Oake Hicory and large Dogwood on the point of a hill, thence S. 24 degrees W. 312 poles to Black Oak poplar and Hicory, thence N. 57 degrees W. 245 poles to the Beginning.

> Dan'l Ashley D. S.
> Surveyed June 18th 1798

Fielding Jones
John Buchannan
John Waggoner, M.   Examined and recorded this 2nd July 1798 by
     C. C.   Young Ewing S. C. C.

A map is at the top front of the document and these notations on the back:

> The Trustees of Bethel Academy 1090 Acres
> Recorded and examined N. 3553   5/414
> Received 28th Nov. '98
> Certified 25th June 1799
> R in Bk 5 Page 414

Note: This record is now kept in the Office of the Secretary of State, of the State of Kentucky in Frankfort, KY, and also on microfilm in the State Library and Archives, Frankfort, KY.

Note on left margin: Francis Poythress; 1090 Acres Christian County N. 819. Examined and Delivered to James Hord 2nd Aug '99.

PATENT #3553

Livingston

Secretary of State, Land Grant Office, Old Kentucky Grants
Book 11, pages 518-519

James Garrard Esquire Governor of the Commonwealth of Kentucky to all to whom these presents shall come greetings. Know ye that by virtue of an act of the Assembly passed the tenth day of February 1798, entitled an act for the endowment of certain Seminaries of learning and for other purposes there is granted by the said Commonwealth unto Francis Poythress, John Kobler, Nathaniel Harris, Barnabas M'Henry, James Croucher, James Howard, John Metcalf and Richard Masterson, Trustees of Bethel Academy for the use and purpose as are proposed in the aforesaid act a certain tract or parcel of land one thousand and ninety acres by survey bearing date eighteenth day of June one thousand seven hundred and ninety-eight lying and being in the County of Christian on a branch of Lost Creek the waters of the Ohio and bounded as followeth, to wit: beginning at a poplar sugar tree and Black Gum running thence North twenty-one degrees East four hundred and thirty-four poles to two Black Oaks and Hickory crossing a branch at two hundred and five one at two hundred and thirty-six poles thence North twenty-one degrees East eighty poles to a Hickory Black Ash and White Oak in the head of a hollow. Thence South seventy degrees East four hundred and twenty poles to sweet gum and two poplars crossing a branch of Lost Creek several times at one hundred and forty poles, thence South twenty-one degrees West two hundred and fifty-two poles to White Oak and Black Ash and Hickory, thence North seventy degrees West one hundred and fifty-six poles to Black Oak Hickory and large Dogwood on the point of a hill, thence South fifty-seven degrees West two hundred and forty-five poles to the beginning with its appurtenances to have and to hold the said tract or parcel of land with its appurtenances to the said Francis Poythress etc. and their successors whereof the said James Garrard Esq. Governor of the Commonwealth of Kentucky hath hereto set his hand and caused the seal of the said Commonwealth to be affixed at Frankfort on the twenty-eighth day of June in the year of our Lord one thousand and ninety-nine and of the Commonwealth of the Eighth.

By the Governor   James Garrard

                       Harry Toulman, Sec't

Notation on the left margin: Francis Poythress 1090 Acres Christian County N. 819. Examined and Delivered to James Hord 2nd Aug '99

Note that Lost Creek in present day Union County is mentioned. See Map #1 showing this stream in the northern part of that county.

The text of the survey and patent of number 5146 #2 follows.

SURVEY 5146 No. 2

Surveyed for the Trustees of Bethel Seminary 800 acres of land by virtue of an Entry made by Daniel Ashley for the Trustees, it being part of said Seminary claims which was taken by Military Claim to wit, off of the 1080 tract taken by David Stephenson survey 62 1/2 acres off of the South East side taken by John Green's survey 737 3/4 off of the 1875 acre tract off of the South East side. In Henderson County on the waters of Cypress a Branch of Tradewater. Beginning at two poplars and Dogwood southwest corner of Robert Curry's survey thence N. 25 degrees W. 334 poles passing Curry's corner at 184 poles to 2 Hickorys and Black Oak on side of a ridge, thence N. 60 degrees E. 260 poles to 3 Ashes and 2 Dogwoods corner of Henry Brandt's Survey, thence N. 15 degrees W. 275 poles to a Black Oak Dogwood and Gum on the side of a hill in Green's Military line, thence with his line S. 45 degrees W. 120 poles to a poplar Dogwood and Elm at corner of Green's Military survey thence S. 45 degrees E. 20 poles to a hickory Dogwood and Elm, thence S. 21 degrees W. 240 poles to a Black Oak and Dogwood, thence N. 45 degrees W. 100 poles to a honey Locust Sycamore White Walnut and Gum corner of Jefferson Seminary thence S. 21 degrees W. 180 poles to a sweet Gum and 2 Dogwoods on the side of a ridge corner of the 265 acre tract of the Bethel Seminary, thence S. 69 degrees E. 170 poles to 3 Black Oak on the top of a hill, thence S. 21 degrees W. 260 poles to 2 Black Oaks thence N. 69 degrees W. 170 poles to White Oaks on the top of a hill, thence S. 21 degrees W. 300 poles to a hickory ash and Elm in Cruppers Military line, thence N. 65 degrees E. 540 poles with said line to the Beginning.

> Surveyed July 20th 1800
> by John Gordon D. S.
> for Edw Talbok S. H. C.

Cyrus Choice
Henry Briant
John Waggoner Mar
    C. C.

A map is at the top right corner of the document and these notations are on the back:

> A plat to the Trustees of Bethel Academy 800 Acres
> Examined and Recorded W. E. T. N. 5146 No. 2
> Received 30th September 1801
> Certified 30th March 1802   7/328

Note: This record is now kept in the Office of the Secretary of State, of the State of Kentucky in Frankfort, KY.

PATENT 2320 (For survey 5146 #2)

Secretary of State, Kentucky Land Office, Old Kentucky Grants

Livingston

Book 14, pages 468-469

James Garrard Esquire Govemor of the Commonwealth of Kentucky to all to whom these presents shall come greetings. Know ye that by virtue and in consideration of an act of the Assembly passed the tenth day of February 1798, entitled an act for the endowment of certain academys of leaming and for other purposes there is granted by the said Commonwealth to the Trustees of Bethel Seminary a certain tract or parcel of land containing Eight hundred acres by survey bearing date the twentieth day of June one thousand eight hundred lying and being in the County of Henderson on the waters of the Cyprus a branch of Tradewater beginning at two Poplars and Dogwood south west comer of Robert Curry's survey running thence North twenty-five degrees West three hundred and thirty-four poles passing Curry's comer at one hundred and eighty-four poles to two hickories and black oak on the side of a ridge thence North sixty degrees East two hundred and sixty poles to three ashes and two Dogwoods comer of Henry Briant's Survey. Thence North fifteen degrees West two hundred and seventy-five poles to a black oak Dogwood and gum on the side of a hill in Green's Military line, thence with his line South forty-five degrees West one hundred and twenty poles to a poplar Dogwood and Elm a comer of Green's Military Survey thence South forty-five degrees East twenty poles to a hickory Dogwood and elm thence South twenty-one degrees West two hundred and forty poles to a Black Oak and Dogwood, thence North forty-five degrees West one hundred poles to a honey locust sycamore white Walnut and gum corner of the Jefferson Seminary thence South twenty-one degrees West one hundred and eighty poles to a sweet gum and two Dogwoods on the side of a ridge comer of the two hundred and sixty-five acre tract of the Bethel Seminary, thence South sixty-nine degrees East one hundred and seventy poles to three black oaks on the top of a hill, thence South twenty-one degrees West two hundred and sixty poles to two black oaks thence North sixty-nine degrees West one hundred and seventy poles to two white oaks on the top of a hill thence South twenty-one degrees West three hundred poles to two hickories ash and elm in Cruppers Military line, thence North sixty-five degrees East five hundred and forty poles with said line to the beginning with its appurtenances to have and to hold the said tract or parcel of land with its appurtenances to the said Trustees of Bethel Academy and their successors forever. In witness whereof the said James Garrard Esq. Govenor of the Commonwealth of Kentucky hath hereunto set his hand and caused the seal of the said Commonwealth to be affixed at Frankfort on the thirtieth day of March in the year of our Lord one thousand and eight hundred and two and of the Commonwealth the Tenth.

By the Govenor James Garrard
Harry Toulman, Secretary of State

Notation on left margin: Bethel Seminary 800 acres Henderson No. 2320

Note that these documents mention Cypress and Tradewater creeks. See map #2 for the location of these creeks in the southern part of Union County.

The text of survey and patent numbered 5985 follows:

SURVEY 5985

Survey for the Trustees of the Bethel Seminary 1000 acres of land by virtue of an entry made by Daniel Ashley for said Trustees in Henderson County on some small branches emptying into the Ohio and bounded as follows, to wit: Beginning at a Hickory Elm and Dogwood corner of Green's Military Survey, running South 21 degrees West 330 poles to a Black oak and Dogwood thence N. 45 degrees W. 500 poles to Black oak and poplar, thence N. 21 degrees E. 330 poles to a stake, thence South 45 degrees East 500 poles to the Beginning.

Surveyed May 20th 1801
By John Gordon D. S.
Edmund Talbot S. H. C.

Fielding Jones
William Harden
        C. C.   Ex'd and Rec'd

Notation: A map of the survey is at the top right of the page and on the back are these data: Bethel Seminary Platt & Cert. 1000 a's. Ex'd and Rec'd Rec'd 10th July 1801 No. 5985 Grant issued 11th January 1808. Recorded Book 8, page 539.

PATENT TO SURVEY 5985
Secretary of State, Kentucky Land Office, Old Kentucky Grants
Book 16, pages 611-612

Christopher Greenup Esquire Governor of the Commonwealth of Kentucky to all whom these presents shall come Greetings. Know ye that by virtue of an act of the Assembly for the endowment of certain seminaries of learning and for other purposes there is granted by the said Commonwealth unto the Trustees of Bethel Seminary, a certain tract or parcel of land containing one thousand acres by survey bearing date the twentieth day of May one thousand eight hundred and seven lying and being in the County of Henderson on some small branches emptying into the Ohio and bounded as followeth, to wit: Beginning at hickory Elm and Dogwood corner of Green's Military survey running South twenty-one West three hundred and thirty poles to a Black oak and dogwood thence North forty-five West five hundred poles to a Black oak and poplar thence North twenty-one East three hundred

Livingston

and thirty poles to a stake thence South forty-five East five hundred poles to the
Beginning with all appurtenances to have and to hold the said tract or parcel of land
with the appurtenances to the said Trustees of Bethel Seminary, and their successors
forever. In Witness whereof the said Christopher Greenup Esquire Governor of the
Commonwealth of Kentucky hath hereunto set his hand and caused the seal of the
said Commonwealth to be affixed at Frankfort on the Eleventh day of January in the
year of our Lord one thousand eight hundred and eight and of the Commonwealth
the sixteenth.

> By the Governor Christo Greenup
> Alfred W. Grayson Secretary

Note: In the upper left margin are these data: Bethel Seminary 1000 acres
>   Henderson County
>   Ex'd and D'd to Daniel Ashley 25th January 1808g

An interesting document among these surveys and patents is survey number 3552
which describes 1,785 acres. The text of this survey is as follows:

SURVEY #3552

Sidebar notation: The Trustees of Bethel Academy, 1785 acres, No. 3552 M, 23
Nov. 98. Missing [followed by a check mark].

Surveyed for Trustees of Bethel Academy [underlined]: Francis Poythress, John
Kobler, Nathaniel Harris, Barnabas McHenry, James Croucher [appears to be a misspelling of Crutcher], James Howard [appears to be a misspelling of Hord], John
Metcalf, and Richard Masterson, and their successors, 1785 acres of land granted by
the legislature of Kentucky to said Trustees and their successors, lying in the County
of Christian [double underline] on the waters of the Ohio [the last two words double underlined], to wit: Beginning at a black oak and poplar, running thence south
45 degrees east 500 poles to black oak and Dogwood, crossing a branch at 400
poles, thence south 45 degrees west 500 poles to two black oaks and Dogwood,
thence north 21 degrees east 600 poles to Black oak, thence south 21 degrees west
600 poles to the Beginning.

> Daniel Ashley D. S.
> Surveyed 21st June 1798

Fielding Jones
>   C. C.
John Buchannan Examined and Received the 2nd July, 1798

John Waggoner M. Young Ewing, S. C. C.

ORIGINAL SURVEY WAS MISSING FROM FILES WHEN RECEIVED FROM THE SEC-
RETARY OF STATE'S OFFICE FROM LAMINATING. A PRINT-BACK COPY OF THE
RECORDED SURVEY IS INCLUDED FOR EASE IN RESEARCH (Also a map of the plat
is missing).

> Sr. The plat and certificate of Eighteen hundred and Seventy-five Acres Surveyed for
> Bethel Academy which is returned to your office appears to clash with prior Claims.
> You are therefore directed not to issue the patents for the Same to Register Land
> Office.
>
> James Hord Trustee
> July 10th 1799

What does the phrase "clash with prior claims" refer to? The names of the surveyor and his
three helpers make up the same team that surveyed numbers 3543, 3551, and 3553
which covered 4,135 acres. The addition of the 1,750 acres of #3552 would total 5,920
acres. Is it possible that this survey overlapped some of the areas of the three previous surveys? Note that both survey #3543, #3551 and #3552 locate their plats on the Ohio
River, which may or may not be tied to the "clash of prior claims."